Addressing the Needs of Returning Women

Linda H. Lewis, *Editor*
University of Connecticut

NEW DIRECTIONS FOR CONTINUING EDUCATION
GORDON G. DARKENWALD, *Editor-in-Chief*
Rutgers University

ALAN B. KNOX, *Consulting Editor*
University of Wisconsin

Number 39, Fall 1988

Paperback sourcebooks in
The Jossey-Bass Higher Education Series

Jossey-Bass Inc., Publishers
San Francisco • London

Ministry of Education, Ontario
Information Centre, 13th Floor,
Mowat Block, Queen's Park,
Toronto, Ont.   M7A 1L2

Linda H. Lewis (ed.).
Addressing the Needs of Returning Women.
New Directions for Continuing Education, no. 39.
San Francisco: Jossey-Bass, 1988.

New Directions for Continuing Education
Gordon G. Darkenwald, *Editor-in-Chief*
Alan B. Knox, *Consulting Editor*

Copyright © 1988 by Jossey-Bass Inc., Publishers
and
Jossey-Bass Limited

Copyright under International, Pan American, and Universal Copyright Conventions. All rights reserved. No part of this issue may be reproduced in any form—except for brief quotation (not to exceed 500 words) in a review or professional work—without permission in writing from the publishers.

New Directions for Continuing Education is published quarterly by Jossey-Bass Inc., Publishers (publication number USPS 493-930). Second-class postage paid at San Francisco, California, and at additional mailing offices. POSTMASTER: Send address changes to Jossey-Bass Inc., Publishers, 350 Sansome Street, San Francisco, California 94104.

Editorial correspondence should be sent to the Editor-in-Chief, Gordon G. Darkenwald, Graduate School of Education, Rutgers University, 10 Seminary Place, New Brunswick, New Jersey 08903.

Library of Congress Catalog Card Number LC 85-644750
International Standard Serial Number ISSN 0195-2242
International Standard Book Number ISBN 1-55542-880-0

Cover art by WILLI BAUM

Manufactured in the United States of America. Printed on acid-free paper.

Ordering Information

The paperback sourcebooks listed below are published quarterly and can be ordered either by subscription or single copy.

Subscriptions cost $52.00 per year for institutions, agencies, and libraries. Individuals can subscribe at the special rate of $39.00 per year *if payment is by personal check.* (Note that the full rate of $52.00 applies if payment is by institutional check, even if the subscription is designated for an individual.) Standing orders are accepted.

Single copies are available at $12.95 when payment accompanies order. (California, New Jersey, New York, and Washington, D.C., residents please include appropriate sales tax.) For billed orders, cost per copy is $12.95 plus postage and handling.

Substantial discounts are offered to organizations and individuals wishing to purchase bulk quantities of Jossey-Bass sourcebooks. Please inquire.

Please note that these prices are for the calendar year 1988 and are subject to change without notice. Also, some titles may be out of print and therefore not available for sale.

To ensure correct and prompt delivery, all orders must give either the *name of an individual* or an *official purchase order number.* Please submit your order as follows:

Subscriptions: specify series and year subscription is to begin.
Single Copies: specify sourcebook code (such as, CE1) and first two words of title.

Mail orders for United States and Possessions, Australia, New Zealand, Canada, Latin America, and Japan to:
Jossey-Bass Inc., Publishers
350 Sansome Street
San Francisco, California 94104

Mail orders for all other parts of the world to:
Jossey-Bass Limited
28 Banner Street
London EC1Y 8QE

New Directions for Continuing Education Series
Gordon G. Darkenwald, *Editor-in-Chief*
Alan B. Knox, *Consulting Editor*

CE1 *Enhancing Proficiencies of Continuing Educators,* Alan B. Knox
CE2 *Programming for Adults Facing Mid-Life Change,* Alan B. Knox
CE3 *Assessing the Impact of Continuing Education,* Alan B. Knox

CE4   *Attracting Able Instructors of Adults,* M. Alan Brown,
      Harlan G. Copeland
CE5   *Providing Continuing Education by Media and Technology,*
      Martin N. Chamberlain
CE6   *Teaching Adults Effectively,* Alan B. Knox
CE7   *Assessing Educational Needs of Adults,* Floyd C. Pennington
CE8   *Reaching Hard-to-Reach Adults,* Gordon G. Darkenwald,
      Gordon A. Larson
CE9   *Strengthening Internal Support for Continuing Education,*
      James C. Votruba
CE10 *Advising and Counseling Adult Learners,* Frank R. DiSilvestro
CE11 *Continuing Education for Community Leadership,* Harold W. Stubblefield
CE12 *Attracting External Funds for Continuing Education,* John H. Buskey
CE13 *Leadership Strategies for Meeting New Challenges,* Alan B. Knox
CE14 *Programs for Older Adults,* Morris A. Okun
CE15 *Linking Philosophy and Practice,* Sharan B. Merriam
CE16 *Creative Financing and Budgeting,* Travis Shipp
CE17 *Materials for Teaching Adults: Selection, Development, and Use,*
      John P. Wilson
CE18 *Strengthening Connections Between Education and Performance,*
      Stanley M. Grabowski
CE19 *Helping Adults Learn How to Learn,* Robert M. Smith
CE20 *Educational Outreach to Select Adult Populations,* Carol E. Kasworm
CE21 *Meeting Educational Needs of Young Adults,* Gordon G. Darkenwald,
      Alan B. Knox
CE22 *Designing and Implementing Effective Workshops,* Thomas J. Sork
CE23 *Realizing the Potential of Interorganizational Cooperation,* Hal Beder
CE24 *Evaluation for Program Improvement,* David Deshler
CE25 *Self-Directed Learning: From Theory to Practice,* Stephen Brookfield
CE26 *Involving Adults in the Educational Process,* Sandra H. Rosenblum
CE27 *Problems and Prospects in Continuing Professional Education,*
      Ronald M. Cervero, Craig L. Scanlan
CE28 *Improving Conference Design and Outcomes,* Paul J. Ilsley
CE29 *Personal Computers and the Adult Learner,* Barry Heermann
CE30 *Experiential and Simulation Techniques for Teaching Adults,*
      Linda H. Lewis
CE31 *Marketing Continuing Education,* Hal Beder
CE32 *Issues in Adult Career Counseling,* Juliet V. Miller, Mary Lynne Musgrove
CE33 *Responding to the Educational Needs of Today's Workplace,* Ivan Charner,
      Catherine A. Rolzinski
CE34 *Technologies for Learning Outside the Classroom,* John A. Niemi,
      Dennis D. Gooler
CE35 *Competitive Strategies for Continuing Education,* Clifford Baden
CE36 *Continuing Education in the Year 2000,* Ralph G. Brockett
CE37 *China: Lessons from Practice,* Wang Maorong, Lin Weihua, Sun Shilu,
      Fang Jing
CE38 *Enhancing Staff Development in Diverse Settings,* Victoria J. Marsick

Contents

Editor's Notes 1
Linda H. Lewis

1. Ingredients of Successful Programming 5
Linda H. Lewis
Principles of good practice are enumerated to assist continuing educators in meeting the needs of returning women.

2. Voices of Returning Women: Ways of Knowing 19
Jill Mattuck Tarule
The ways in which returning women experience the learning environment provide an alternate perspective both on women's development and on their educational experiences.

3. Returning Women on Campus: 35
Higher Education Takes Notice
Barbara A. Copland
The response of postsecondary institutions to returning women is demonstrated through case examples of viable models and effective programs.

4. Supporting Women's Reentry to the Workplace 49
Karen E. Watkins
Innovative practices and programs in business and industry demonstrate how the workplace is adopting supportive work structures and benefits that encourage women's participation.

5. Community-Based Training for Reentry Women 65
in Nontraditional Occupations
Ruth S. Howell, Helen Schwartz
The unique strengths of community-based organizations are evidenced by the variety of special services and opportunities made available to women training for nontraditional fields.

6. Women from Special Populations: 79
The Challenge of Reentry
Phyllis C. Safman
Case studies illuminate the psychosocial characteristics of special populations of reentry women, the barriers they face, and their unique needs.

7. Extending an Invitation to Returning Women 95
Linda H. Lewis

The essence of the reentry experience is captured through both poetry and prose as returning women's experiences, needs, and concerns are described and summarized.

Index 111

Editor's Notes

One of the most notable trends in the last two decades has been the dramatic increase in continuing education among nontraditional-aged females. Such factors as the human potential movement, changing demographic profiles, inflation, advanced technology, divorce, and growth in the number of one-parent and dual-career households have prompted participation by women who had previously deferred career preparation, college, or continuing education. In addition, women's development of political consciousness, greater self-awareness, and need to be self-supporting are other factors that have affected women's life patterns and spurred women's participation in education and work.

The magnitude of women's reentry is evidenced in the statistical profiles of their continuing education enrollment. According to the most recent census, women accounted for 55 percent of the total number of participants in adult education nationwide (Hill, 1987). In postsecondary education, the number of women over twenty-five returning to school has increased almost tenfold in the past twenty years as reentry women have become the largest group of new students to fill the gap created by the declining number of traditional-aged students (U.S. Bureau of the Census, 1984). In large measure, this growth in enrollment is due to the participation or reenrollment of women, who outnumber men two to one among people thirty-five and over and whose attendance at postsecondary institutions exceeds that of males. Currently, women over twenty-five make up 42 percent of all part-time enrollment in higher education (Snyder, 1987), and it is estimated that by the year 2000, 52 percent of all undergraduate students will be women, with 50 percent of these twenty-two and older (Carnegie Council on Policy Studies in Higher Education, 1980). Such statistical profiles and projections not only help to characterize the environment of the 1980s and 1990s but also impress upon program planners, administrators, instructors, and counselors the need to develop programs to service this burgeoning population. Many schools and businesses have actively recruited, developed, and expanded services for returning women, but the need to design responsive programming and ensure access for reentry women still exists. Despite commitments to outreach and to the provision of special services, the issues facing returning women are neither obsolete nor resolved. Given the dramatic changes in the educational profile over the last few decades, now is a compelling time for continuing education to take a fresh look at this new majority. Renewed efforts need to be initiated to change institutional structures and build agendas that truly promote access, equity, and support for reentry women.

The purpose of this sourcebook is to assist continuing educators in meeting the needs of nontraditional women students. A conceptual framework to define the social context of returning women's participation, their characteristics, and concerns will give readers a fuller understanding of the relevant issues confronting reentry women. Examples of successful practices in postsecondary education, business and industry, and community-based organizations are presented through case studies, each of which has relevance and transferability for practitioners seeking to facilitate the continuing development of returning women.

Chapter One sets the frame of reference for the volume by sensitizing readers to the heterogeneity of returning women and the differences that exist in their motivations and their readiness to engage in organized learning. The characteristics and concerns of reentry women provide the backdrop for describing the effective practices and appropriate strategies that institutions, agencies, and businesses can implement to facilitate women's successful transition into an educational setting.

Chapter Two provides insights into the diverse ways in which reentry women experience the learning environment. Their adult voices serve as a paradigm for understanding the learning needs of the reentry woman and the meaning she makes of our pedagogical and programmatic efforts.

Chapters Three, Four, and Five provide case examples from higher education, business, and community-based organizations that illustrate how each sector is striving to meet the needs of returning women. The respective chapters demonstrate how responsive programming and innovative practices can encourage women's continuing participation in organized learning.

Chapter Six focuses on women from special populations, including displaced homemakers, rural dwellers, minorities, and the disabled. Cultural and ethnic diversity, as well as environmental and situational variables, are the basis for defining the needs of specific reentry populations.

Chapter Seven begins with a poem commissioned especially for this volume. It characterizes the reentry experience of some women. Besides providing an editorial summary and resource information, the final chapter calls attention to the pivotal role played by significant others who have an impact on the continuing and successful participation of returning women.

References

Carnegie Council on Policy Studies in Higher Education. *Three Thousand Futures: The Next Twenty Years for Higher Education.* San Francisco: Jossey-Bass, 1980.

Hill, S. T. *Trends in Adult Education: 1969-1984.* Washington, D.C.: Center for Education Statistics, 1987.

Snyder, D. T. *Digest of Educational Statistics.* Washington, D.C.: Center for Education Statistics, 1987.

U.S. Bureau of the Census. *Statistical Abstract of the U.S.* (104th ed.) Washington, D.C.: U.S. Government Printing Office, 1984.

Linda H. Lewis is an associate professor of adult education at the University of Connecticut and codirector of the university's Vocational Equity Research, Training, and Evaluation Center.

When individual support is boosted by institutional commitment, reentry women reap maximum benefits.

Ingredients of Successful Programming

Linda H. Lewis

Defining the term *reentry* is key to any discussion of returning women. While a variety of adjectives can easily be applied to profile the characteristics of this distinctive population, the reality is that no one individual may approximate the archetype that is created. In fact, returning women may differ markedly in the degree to which any combination of identified attributes is actually characteristic. Commonly accepted definitions, however, conceive of a reentry woman as someone who left school to take a job or assume family responsibilities, but who is currently seeking to return to school or work. Returning women are diverse in their socioeconomic backgrounds and run the gamut in their educational and career continuity and discontinuity. They range in age from twenty-five to over sixty-five, with the majority between twenty-five and fifty. They may be single, divorced, married, or widowed, with or without children. Sometimes referred to as dropouts, stopouts, empty-nesters, second or ongoing careerists, homemakers, or veterans, the naming alone says more

---

Many thanks to Dellene Watt Quintilliani, whose commencement speech, contained in this chapter, may inspire others contemplating a return to school. Dellene has recently been accepted into the University of Connecticut's School of Social Work and is a strong proponent of continuing education.

about those describing returning women than it does about the women themselves.

At one time, continuing education was considered to be a middle-class phenomenon, but this is no longer the case. Returning women may be working class, economically deprived, upwardly mobile, or upper class. Some may have been absent from an educational setting for more than thirty-five years, while others simply left briefly to assume family responsibilities or pursue employment. Within reentry populations, there are many diverse and special-needs groups, including minorities, older women, displaced homemakers, disabled women, single parents, rural, and low-income women. Thus, the size and composition of a reentry population may imply the need for very different or even divergent responses on the part of institutions, agencies, employers, and continuing education programs.

Reentry Then and Now

In the 1970s, discussions about returning women focused on boredom, self-fulfillment, and career preparation as the prime motivators of women's return to educational settings (Astin, 1976; Durcholz and O'Conner, 1976). Research did mention women who were going back to school to fulfill personal goals, or who were interested in finding more stimulating or better-paying jobs, but such individuals were minimally accounted for in the literature (Astin, 1976). Instead, the emphasis was on pioneers who dared to deviate from the norm and venture forth from domestic tranquility, or on women whose futures were dictated by economic necessity. It is now clear that early researchers identified only a few of the motives for women's return to educational programs.

Clayton and Smith (1987) help us to broaden our understanding of why women return to formal education. Confirming and expanding on earlier research (Maslin, 1978), they describe a similarity in motive patterns that exists across population samples of reentry women. Their findings help to debunk previous hypotheses: that the empty-nest syndrome is the primary reason for women's return to school or work, or that there is a single dominant positive motive for women's engaging in continuing education. Rather, the reasons for participation are broadly based, ranging from the need to gain a new perspective on one's marital role and responsibilities to meeting social expectations. Returning women commonly identify needs to become financially self-supporting, to expand and grow, to raise self-esteem, to learn about life and the world, to take pride in their achievements, to prepare for employment, and to increase their chances of being hired or promoted (Clayton and Smith, 1987). Issues related to role and family expectations (the need not to be absorbed by home demands and to be able to provide enriching intellectual and financial resources for one's family), along with social and humanitarian drives (to make others proud, to share knowledge, to benefit others, and to meet new people), describe additional motive types (Clayton and Smith, 1987).

The purpose of enumerating the multiple reasons for women's reentry is threefold. First, the extensive list points out how difficult it is to characterize or stereotype returning women. There are no definitive statements that can be made about the motives and sociodemographic variables (Maslin, 1978). Second, whatever her motivation, each reentry woman brings her own unique traits, assets, and problems with her to her educational world. Third, enumerating the reasons for women's reentry impresses educational providers with the necessity of developing a variety of programs to satisfy the often unique and diverse needs of this population.

While this extensive list provides insights into why a woman might return to school, it is important to bear in mind that the timing for her return is not solely a function of motivation but is related to the state of relationships and occurrences in her daily life. What propels an individual to enroll at a particular point is a complex interaction of life events, personal motivation, and goals (Mahoney and Anderson, 1988).

Balancing Multiple Roles. Multiple role responsibility characterizes reentry women of the 1980s and is a trait that helps to distinguish them from traditional-aged students. While a traditional-aged student's primary role is that of student, many returning women must combine student status with the responsibilities of being a wife, mother, significant other, wage earner, community member, and any combination thereof. The epithet *superwoman* has exacerbated the situation by suggesting that "doing it all" is something toward which to strive. The prevailing assumption of the literature, however, is that—despite the sense of self-worth that often accompanies a return to school—strain, anxiety, and stress are the inevitable consequences of multiple role incumbency (Greenhaus and Beutell, 1985). Many returning women are pulled in several (and often conflicting) directions by a seemingly endless stream of demands from work, family, friends, and community. Identity-line tension, the point of discomfort where new definitions of gender roles threaten other aspects of an individual's life, is not uncommon when conflicts occur as a result of a female's return to an educational setting (Yogev, 1983). For example, it is not unusual that significant others (friends, spouses, family members, employers) are threatened by or opposed to a woman's educational or career pursuits (Lewis, 1983). For returning women, lack of time to devote to family, home, and domestic responsibilities can result in the need to develop a wide range of coping behaviors in order to maintain existing relationships and avoid conflict while still allowing women to incorporate their ethic of caring for others (Gilligan, 1982). The situation is particularly difficult for single parents, who, in addition to coping with financial difficulties, may still encounter social disapproval on the basis of their marital status.

Thus, for many women, reentry is a transitional time, when the presence or absence of institutional and personal support can make the difference between continuing participation and dropping out. The priority that many women place on considering relationships when making decisions may help to explain such sequences as partial education, marriage, birth of children, more education, and career involvement that have traditionally characterized women's lives. As the linear staging of life patterns and career decisions is reevaluated by today's women, however, the availability of educational supports is vital for helping individuals better evaluate their commitments, manage their roles, and affirm the validity of their undertakings.

Personal Concerns. Women who want to reenter learning environments confront a number of personal concerns that may affect their participation. Sometimes referred to as personal and situational barriers (Cross, 1981), these factors can be due to a woman's personal circumstances, the situation in which she finds herself, her self-image, or the demands she places on herself.

Many returning women express self-doubt about their ability to compete with younger students, who have more recent educational experience. For some, lower levels of academic self-confidence are the result of earlier experiences in home environments where education was not valued. The sparse use of talents in rewarding settings, or the absence of feedback about one's real abilities, may have contributed to increasing some women's anxieties about their ability to perform. For others, who may have married early, high school education and modest to nonexistent occupational histories may contribute to anxieties about potential to succeed in educational settings (Chickering and Havighurst, 1981).

Prior achievement does not seem to have any benefit, because concerns about rusty study skills (note taking, exam preparation) and ability to keep up (memorize, remember facts) often take precedence (Maccoby and Jacklin, 1974). Unfortunately, part-time students are sometimes considered to be less serious about education or peripheral to an institution. Students who do not attend full-time may be viewed as uncommitted, as frivolous, or as seeking fulfillment, rather than as taking their studies in earnest (Hall, 1981). Attitudes reflecting a "climate of unexpectation"—questioning the seriousness with which women students are pursuing education—serve only to increase feelings of intimidation (Dickerson and Hinkle, 1979). The reality, however, is that despite their initial tentativeness, individual reentry students earn higher grades when they return to school than they did when previously enrolled (Hall, 1981). Moreover, when compared to traditional female students, reentry women also have higher grades (Leppell, 1984).

Many returning women express concerns about their physical appearance. Feeling that they may appear out of place, different, or improperly dressed, they often try to accommodate to the demands of what they perceive to be a youth-oriented environment. Certainly, being older means generational differences and physical changes, but the issues facing women in midlife go far beyond these factors. Returning women have introspective concerns that are based on their own mental and emotional states. These concerns may center on financial pressures, on changing life roles as mothers or wives, on the realization that there is a finite amount of time remaining to accomplish goals, or on feelings of guilt that sometimes accompany a return to school.

Concerns about childcare, especially when preschool children are involved, are enormous. A study at one university revealed that one-third of the women students who were dissatisfied with their childcare arrangements said they would increase their course loads an average of 3.6 credits per term if that could resolve childcare problems. Another third indicated having withdrawn for an average of 1.7 terms because of difficulties with childcare (Creange, 1981). For women returning to school, obtaining high-quality childcare may mean the difference between dropping out and taking additional classes. Not only do a large number of reentry women have children, but many in their late twenties and thirties, who previously delayed childbearing, will be competing for childcare services in the coming decade. The problem for many of these women is that neighbors or others who would have cared for children in the past are themselves returning to the labor force and are thus unavailable to provide childcare.

Many displaced homemakers and single parents, already struggling to make ends meet, lack the resources to pay for their educations as well as the care of their children. There are over 11,431,000 displaced homemakers in the United States (Displaced Homemakers Network, 1987). These are women whose principal job has been homemaker, but who have lost their main source of income because of divorce, separation, widowhood, or the long-term disability of a spouse. In addition, there are over 3,223,000 single parents who would be in the displaced-homemaker category if they were not employed full-time. Despite their employment status, however, three-quarters of all single-parent families are living below the income level at which the Department of Labor estimates day-to-day living expenses can be met. The number of single parents with minor children, coupled with the fact that nearly one-fourth of the nation's displaced homemakers have children under eighteen in their care, makes it become obvious that there are subgroups of special-need reentry populations for whom childcare is a critical issue (Displaced Homemakers Network, 1987). The situation is only compounded when one considers that childcare is also a pressing need for returning women from intact nuclear families.

Many returning women will ask for help and support, but others will not. The need for services that provide orientation, assimilation, counseling, support, financial aid, and childcare cannot be overestimated, yet it is obvious that differences in reentry populations will necessitate varying student personnel policies and approaches. While this chapter is intended to provide readers with a profile of returning women, their concerns, and their needs, there is no better way to provide a composite picture than to hear from a reentry woman herself. The following is the commencement address written by Dellene Watt Quintilliani, a mother of five who, after an absence of twenty-five years, returned to school to obtain a college degree. Although very much a personal statement, her remarks epitomize the concerns and anxieties described earlier in this chapter, as well as the remarkable transition from fear to self-confidence that so often occurs.

As I stand here this morning, my thoughts go back to a fall day four years ago. My stomach churned. I felt terrified. Nothing I put on looked right. My skirt looked too dressy, my jeans too sloppy. I settled for a turtleneck shirt, sweater, and corduroy slacks. The drive to the university takes twenty minutes from my home, but I left an hour early, as I did not want to be late for my very first class.

Being a nontraditional student was difficult enough; I did not want to draw attention to myself by being late. By the way, whatever *nontraditional student* means to some of you, for me it meant not only that I was old enough to be the parent of most of my peers, your sons and daughters, but also that I had the pleasure of paying tuition bills for my children as well as myself.

Arriving on campus, I walked toward Dana Hall, where I would take my first class—Psychology 110. My blue backpack was slung over one shoulder, as backpacks are supposed to be. Having five children, I was acutely aware that backpacks are always slung over one shoulder, not to ease or balance the load but rather to look "in" or cool. My concern was not whether or not I looked "in," but I certainly did not want to look any more "out" than was absolutely necessary. Being invisible would have been ideal.

I entered a large auditorium, seated myself in the front row, and waited. It had been twenty-five years since I had experienced any formal education. I felt joyous at the prospect of being an integral part of this university, but terrified that I could not survive academically.

As students trickled in, I thought of my own five children and how nice it would be to spend time with young people who did not have peanut butter and jelly on their hands or for whose bills and antics I would not feel responsible. However, I recognized that my peers came to the university armed with recent quiz and test scores—SATs, APs, and

Stanley Kaplan experiences. I had never taken an SAT or an AP, and my single experience with Stanley Kaplan was writing a check for my son to take a preparatory course.

My anxiety level increased as students entered the classroom and the clock ticked onward. At 10:30 A.M. sharp, Dr. Wallace, a formidable-looking man dressed in a navy blue blazer and sharply creased gray flannel slacks, entered the auditorium. I wanted to flee but felt riveted to my seat. Dr. Wallace nodded slightly and smiled, easing my tension. That moment is vividly etched in my memory. It was the moment I had long awaited, the moment my education would begin.

I attended classes daily, and October arrived quickly. My first exam was scheduled that month, and the terror I had felt on the first day of classes returned. The morning of the exam arrived, and I left for the university an hour early, as I always did, but this day was different. This day I cried all the way to the university. I cried because I was afraid to take the exam and fail. I was afraid to try. I knew that if I chose not to take the exam, I could always say to myself, "Dellene, you could have passed the exam, you simply chose not to take it." But I also knew that if I chose not to take that exam, my hopes for an education, my dream of a diploma, would vanish. Somehow I could not turn back to the past—back to those feelings of inadequacy and insecurity. I walked toward Dana Hall as I had every Monday, Wednesday, and Friday for weeks.

As the exam and blue books were distributed, a feeling of panic engulfed me. For some of you, a blue book is a small guidebook that car dealers produce, showing proof positive that your used car is not worth nearly as much as you had hoped. But for university students, blue books are passed out with exams, and in them we attempt to convince professors that we know more than we actually do. I was surprised that I understood the questions and knew the answers—not all of them, but most. I felt exhilarated, ecstatic that I had finally found the courage to risk failure. That was the beginning of my courage and my real education.

As I joined my peers, I had strong ideas about what education would mean and what it would do for me. My expectations were that professors would present information and share their knowledge, and I would attend classes and learn. I would be filled with knowledge, just as a baby bottle is filled with formula, and presto, education would occur. I could not have been more wrong.

Education has been a long road with forks, intersections, and green lights, and with an end undisclosed because there isn't one. I have traveled in partnership with bright and caring instructors who encouraged me, cajoled me, and demanded that I give my best. These individuals were adept at facilitating class discussions, always insisting that I learn to think, to reason, and to question. It was not sufficient to give professors back the knowledge they had articulately given me; rather, I had to question information, consider alternatives, and examine long-held but rarely questioned beliefs.

This morning I scrambled out of bed long before the alarm sounded. Four years had passed since I came to this university, and today, the day I had dreamed about, had finally arrived. Today I was going to graduate. My stomach churned, and I felt anxious. But today was different. My anxiety reflected the joy and anticipation of this moment. I searched my closet looking for the proper outfit, but the need to blend in—to be almost invisible—did not exist. I wanted to look like me, Dellene, the person I am.

Leaving my home for the twenty-minute drive to the university, an hour early as always, I realized that the terror of failure was gone. The challenge was in finding the courage to risk failure. I have met that challenge, and today I take that courage with me.

Institutional Barriers. Once a woman makes the decision to continue her education, the implementation of her plan is not always easy. There are numerous obstacles that can be imposed by institutions, programs, or individuals that can be as powerful as a woman's own internal constraints. School policies, for example, can have a direct effect by either helping or hindering women's participation.

While many schools have devised appropriate admissions policies, eligibility requirements continue to be an issue for many women seeking entry into degree-granting institutions. Examinations such as the Scholastic Aptitude Test, the Miller Analogies Test, and Graduate Record Examination are intimidating requirements for those who have been away from school for many years. When requested to submit letters of recommendation, returning women may be faced with the fact that those who could write such letters are no longer around or do not remember them. Credits taken over the years may be too old to be transferable, making it necessary for returning women to repeat courses. According to the U.S. Census Bureau, the average American moves 12.9 times during a lifetime, and 50 percent of the U.S. population moves every five years (Fisher-Thompson, 1981). Given this situation, few will be able to demonstrate an orderly progression of educational experiences. It is also likely that the specific courses needed for graduation will not be identical to those required by schools previously attended. Although credit for prior learning and life experiences is a logical alternative, the practice is still not widespread. Add to this list residency requirements and artificial time limits for completing degrees, and once again returning women are at a disadvantage. A woman who cannot attend school full-time, because she must work to support her family or because her responsibilities at home preclude a full-time load, may never enroll in the first place, may drop out, or may postpone her studies until she can attend full-time (Fisher-Thompson, 1981).

Much of what can be said about institutional barriers applies equally to all nontraditional adult students. For part-time learners to participate, their access to facilities, learning resources, administrative offices, study-skill centers, employment, placement, and food services is crucial. Bookstores or continuing education offices that are open only during traditional weekday hours make things extremely difficult for those who are employed. Parking restrictions that limit permits and spaces to full-time students also place part-time students in a peripheral position. Traditional class schedules, without flexible weekend or evening options; absence of outreach or off-campus locations; lack of childcare: these are all policies that can bar classes to potential returning students. Moreover, financial aid becomes a conundrum for women who have only enough money to attend part-time, but who, because of their less than half-time status, are ineligible for tuition assistance. Major federal aid programs, including work study, have been made available to at least half-time students, but full time students are often given preference over returning women, whose seriousness and "need" are questioned (Hall, 1981).

Studies comparing returning women to other nontraditional students find that reentry women are less likely to use support services (Kasworm, 1980; Bandenhoop and Johansen, 1980). Many women feel that they must handle the transition themselves. They avoid student services, feeling that these are designed for traditional students. Many institutions and programs do extend support services geared specifically to part-time or returning students, but often publicity and information about such programs do not find their way to the target audience. Lack of funds, the absence of a dedicated position to assist reentry students, and the absence of literature on returning women can contribute to lack of awareness about and underuse of support services.

This discussion has focused on institutional barriers to participation, but numerous practices can be instituted to facilitate the transition and participation of reentry women. The following suggestions are offered as a checklist for good practice and can be used by anyone who wants to make a commitment to the success of women returning to educational settings.

Thirty Ways to Facilitate Reentry

1. Initiate campaigns to attract reentry women. Develop strategies and materials for reaching potential women students and special-needs reentry populations (single parents, displaced homemakers, minorities, older women).

2. Publish handbooks, newsletters, and newspapers designed to meet the needs of returning women that contain tips from other reentry women.

3. Disseminate literature about offerings and programs throughout the community to places that are frequented by potential returning women (childcare centers, doctors' offices, churches and synagogues, laundromats, supermarkets, public assistance offices).

4. Develop spot announcements for radio and television and place ads in local newspapers to attract returning women.

5. Organize conferences and special days for reentry women, for those who are considering continuing education or who have made previous contacts. Include other reentry women as recruiters and encourage peer counseling.

6. Set up special telephone lines that returning students can call evenings and weekends for course and enrollment information.

7. Establish extended hours for administrative offices and support services.

8. Develop training to sensitize teachers and staff who will be working with returning women, so that they can provide better service.

9. Identify reentry liaisons who are willing to serve as contacts for returning women, and publish their names in a directory for potential or newly enrolled women.

10. Evaluate women's childcare needs and, as necessary, provide a variety of childcare services (cooperative arrangements with other schools or businesses, evening and weekend care).

11. Set up registration processes to ensure that part-time returning women will have access to the classes they need.

12. Conduct specially designed orientation sessions that returning women are strongly encouraged to attend, and review financial aid eligibility, describe support services, and respond to questions.

13. Hold special receptions and open houses to introduce reentry women to women's networks, career opportunities, and reentry peers.

14. Offer preadmission and career counseling to assist prospective returning women students in decision making.

15. Offer a wide range of basic skills and refresher courses, at convenient times and locations, geared to the specific concerns of returning women. Provide self-paced individualized instructional programs, guidebooks, cassettes, and videos to enable women to brush up at home on their study skills.

16. Set aside scholarships for needy returning women students who do not qualify for federal aid, and provide lists of private organizations and corporate sponsors that offer financial assistance.

17. Develop tuition incentive programs, along with "givebacks" for those who have other family members enrolled in an educational program.

18. On the basis of the services that reentry women are interested in using, develop flexible payment plans and policies for increasing or reducing fees.

19. Allow for the fulfillment of residency requirements through part-time enrollment, internships, practica, and independent study.

20. Provide lounges and designated meeting places where returning women and other commuters can socialize with peers.

21. Reserve centrally located parking for part-time students, and publicize the availability of commuter or minibus services that are offered by the school, community organizations, or municipal departments.

22. Provide short-term and emergency housing for part-time returning women who travel long distances.

23. Facilitate the development of support groups for returning women to discuss issues of personal concern.

24. Provide counseling services that help women look realistically at their options, life plans, personal growth, and career development.

25. Develop support services to alleviate the developmental stress for women who are at different stages in the reentry process, as well as in their own lives.

26. Provide flexible and varied scheduling options by offering courses once a week, late afternoons, or evenings. Explore options such as innovative weekend programs, internships, external degree programs, and modular courses.

27. Offer a variety of options to encourage participation, such as noncredit, pass/fail, and conditional admission.

28. Encourage instructors to be available at nontraditional times and to establish telephone hours for those who are unable to meet in person.

29. Redesign requirements so as to eliminate artificial criteria that adversely affect returning women. To assess potential, use other evaluative criteria: volunteer experience, committee membership, autobiographical statements, portfolios of past experience, self-report, and self-evaluation.

30. Evaluate the content and style of questions on information forms to ensure that they are not biased against mature women (for example, "Parents' Names and Address[es]").

To ensure that programs for returning women are responsive to this population, periodic evaluation is a must. Given the general rate of change today, reentry populations can also be expected to change. At one time, childcare may be an overriding concern, but changing demographic profiles or increased governmental support for daycare facilities may make it necessary to reevaluate priorities. Committees will need to be established, not only to evaluate the effectiveness and appropriateness of what already exists, but also to assess emerging needs and concerns. Nevertheless, the ultimate success of continuing education for returning women rests on institutional credibility. Evaluations of successful programs suggests that women's reentry is facilitated only to the extent that programs receive encouragement and support from top-level administrators (Whatley, 1975). Regardless of a program's potential, it will be perceived as marginal if it is not somehow incorporated into a visible substructure. The sad reality is that programs perceived as peripheral can undermine women's feelings of inclusion, involvement, and solidarity. Support for such programs is vital for the establishment of returning women as a visible, credible, and significant cohort of adult learners. Placement of programs, services, and activities in successful, well-established divisions, which can serve either as sponsors or delegators, is a statement that returning women are a valued constituency supported by those with decision-making power (Grottkau, 1988). Only when individual support is boosted by institutional commitment can we boast of having truly responded to the needs of returning women.

References

Astin, H. S. *Some Action of Her Own: The Adult Woman and Higher Education.* Lexington, Mass.: Heath, 1976.

Bandenhoop, M. S., and Johansen, M. K. "Do Re-entry Women Have Special Needs?" *The Counseling Psychologist,* 1980, *4,* 491-595.

Chickering, A., and Havighurst, R. "The Life Cycle." In A. W. Chickering (ed.), *The Modern American College: Responding to the New Realities of Diverse Students and a Changing Society.* San Francisco: Jossey-Bass, 1981.

Clayton, D. E., and Smith, M. M. "Motivational Typology of Reentry Women." *Adult Education Quarterly,* 1987, *37* (2), 90-104.

Creange, R. *Campus Child Care: A Challenge for the 80's.* Washington, D.C.: Project on the Status and Education of Women, Association of American Colleges, 1981.

Cross, K. P. *Adults as Learners: Increasing Participation and Facilitating Learning.* San Francisco: Jossey-Bass, 1981.

Dickerson, K. G., and Hinkle, D. E. "Entering Freshman Women's Expectations of Support and Encouragement at the University." *Journal of National Association of Women Deans, Administrators and Counselors,* 1979, *43* (1), 8-12.

Displaced Homemakers Network. *A Status Report on Displaced Homemakers and Single Parents in the United States.* Washington, D.C.: Displaced Homemakers Network, 1987.

Durcholz, P., and O'Conner, J. "Why Women Go Back to College." *Change,* 1976, *5* (8), 52-56.

Fisher-Thompson, J. *An Overview of Re-entry Women: Meeting the Enrollment Challenge.* Washington, D.C.: Project on the Status and Education of Women, 1981.

Gilligan, C. *In a Different Voice.* Cambridge, Mass.: Harvard University Press, 1982.

Greenhaus, J. H., and Beutell, N. J. "Sources of Conflict Between Work and Family Roles." *Academy of Management Review,* 1985, *10,* 76-88.

Grottkau, B. "P.E.E.R.S.: Programming Experiences for Returning Students." *Lifelong Learning,* 1988, *11* (4), 10-13.

Hall, R. *Re-entry Women: Part-Time Enrollment, Full-Time Commitment.* Washington, D.C.: Project on the Status and Education of Women, Association of American Colleges, 1981.

Kasworm, C. E. "Student Services for the Older Undergraduate Student." *Journal of College Student Personnel,* 1980, *21* (2), 163-169.

Leppell, K. "The Academic Performance of Returning and Continuing College Students: An Economic Analysis." *Journal of Economic Education*, 1984, *15*, 46-54.

Lewis, L. H. "Coping with Change: Married Women in Graduate School." *Lifelong Learning*, 1983, 7 (1), 8-28.

Maccoby, E., and Jacklin, C. *The Psychology of Sex Differences*. Stanford, Calif.: Stanford University Press, 1974.

Mahoney, C., and Anderson, W. "The Effect of Life Events and Relationships on Adult Women's Decisions to Enroll in College." *Journal of Counseling and Development*, 1988, *66*, 271-274.

Maslin, A. "Older Undergraduate Women at an Urban University: A Typology of Motives, Ego Development, Sextypedness, and Attitude Toward Women's Role." Doctoral dissertation, Temple University, 1978.

Whatley, A. E. "Continuing Education for Women: Gaining Institutional Credibility." *Journal of National Association of Women Deans, Administrators and Counselors*, 1975, *39*, 9-15.

Yogev, S. "Judging the Professional Woman: Changing Research, Changing Values." *Psychology of Women Quarterly*, 1983, 7 (3), 219-234.

Linda H. Lewis is an associate professor of adult education at the University of Connecticut and codirector of the university's Vocational Equity Research, Training, and Evaluation Center.

Three perspectives on adult women's development and experience of learning suggest new dimensions to consider in designing appropriate programs for returning women students.

Voices of Returning Women: Ways of Knowing

Jill Mattuck Tarule

In the film *Educating Rita*, Rita arrives at her mentor's office, teetering through the halls of academe on spike heels, her hair bleached blonde, her speech peppered with cockney slang. She is a picture of incongruity, an inappropriate student among the "ivy" of the academy. Her first approach to education is both metaphorically and actually awkward and embarrassing as she flies into the room when the sticky latch on her professor's door finally gives way. The mentor's approach to his new adult student is an equally powerful metaphor. He is reluctant to become her tutor, partly because he is mired in self doubt and alcohol, but his major complaint is the inconvenience of having to remain after hours to accommodate Rita.

It is noteworthy that an adult woman beginning or returning to formal education, or simply wanting to learn, is enough of a cultural anomaly to make Rita's story reasonable literary material (Shaw, 1981; Bryant, 1982). Statistically, however, these anomalies have nearly become commonplace in academic environments, which are often insensitive to the particular needs of returning women. This chapter examines perspectives on what some of those needs might be, drawing on two sources: adult women's stories about their education, and theory about women's learning.

Belenky and others (1986) explore how women learn, as well as women's experience and definition of the educational environments in which they find themselves. Based on this work, three perspectives for understanding adult women students will be discussed. The first perspective is that of *voice*, which refers to the ability to articulate one's sense of self and supports the individual as she develops a sense of identity, efficacy, and competence. The second perspective is that of *connected knowing* and how it influences both the way the individual reasons and what she experiences as important in her learning environment. The third perspective is that of the student's *developmental position*, which influences how she learns and understands what knowledge is, how she relates to teachers and peers, and how she experiences her purposes in becoming educated.

Each perspective corresponds, respectively, to what have been considered desirable outcomes of education. Gaining and having a voice refers to the ability to articulate considered positions and to the capacity to be a confident knower who has mastered the means of enhanced participation in a social and political community. Developing as a connected learner can liberate a woman from previous constraints on her self-definition as a knower and can enhance her ability to participate in and contribute to scholarship and critical analysis. Finally, developmental position indicates the potential for furthering increased complexity in understanding and thinking. Thus, we can consider each perspective both as an aspect of the returning student's experience and as a realm of influence on educational practice that intends particular outcomes.

Voice, connected learning, and developmental position are explored in depth in Belenky and others (1986). Here, these perspectives will be summarized and followed by an examination of how each one helps our understanding of the returning student. Data on adult women are drawn from literature and from the present author's two decades of teaching returning adults, mostly women.

The concept of voice as the capacity to speak up about how one understands and makes meaning of the world is a recurrent theme in women's stories of their development. Women have been identified as speaking in a "different voice" from that of the majority culture (Gilligan, 1982), as employing different strategies in dialogue, and as having a particular sensitivity and ability to engage in conversation that is exploratory rather than decisive. While completed ideas—bulletins from one's thinking—may be the norm for conversations in the academy, women students enter the educational setting with well-developed abilities to hold their opinions silent while they question another person about hers (interviewing); to engage in narrative conversations that trace the details ("Then he said; then she said"); and to remain sensitive to how well a message is being received by checking with the listener (such as by using a tag question at the end of a statement: "Did that make sense to you?") (Kramarae, 1981; Hall and Sandler, 1982). In interviews with women students of all ages, the metaphor of voice as a descriptor for women's sense of themselves is inextricably interwoven with women's experience of themselves as learning and as thinking, as having minds at all (Belenky and others, 1986).

In addition to the metaphor of voice, women describe a preferred mode of learning that defines a set of strategies for acquiring new ideas, whether from a text, a peer, or a teacher (Belenky and others, 1986). In regard to reasoning, the connected learner emphasizes understanding and acceptance of an idea as a strategy that, at the very least, ought to precede if not replace the more common strategy of assessment or criticism. Thus, cooperative or collaborative discussions about ideas are preferred over argumentative debates. Such discussions often allow for a respectful inclusion of firsthand experience in the project of becoming knowledgeable: the personal is included in the process of making meaning in one's learning (Belenky and others, 1986). As women describe their learning and what works for them in education, they assert that the development of authentic voice has been most supported when learning has emphasized opportunities to make connections, rather than when it has emphasized a weeding out the self as the objective and only way to learn.

At the heart of a preference for connected learning is the value and importance of making and maintaining relationships of all kinds. What emerges from descriptions of connected learning is a perspective on the educational enterprise that highlights the personal and experiential, as well as relationships between oneself and the material, between oneself and the teacher, and between what one learns and how one is living one's life. This perspective permeates both how the environment is experienced and how the student undertakes analysis.

In her thinking, the connected learner uses a series of considerations as a particular cognitive strategy, one that is distinct from separate learning strategies. Two quotes illustrate these differences.

"I never take anything I read or that someone says at face value. I just tend to see the contrary I like playing devil's advocate, arguing the opposite of what someone is saying, thinking of exceptions to what the person has said, or thinking of a different train of thought" (Belenky and others, 1986, p. 100). This woman plays what Elbow (1973) calls "the doubting game." She looks for what is wrong, separates herself from the argument, and works at seeing how she can frame an opposing position. She stresses what is missing and what might be added to the idea. Her academic work may well have a high level of clarity. It is often astute, and it involves what we have traditionally defined as both critical thinking and as an appropriate outcome of education.

In contrast, a connected learner describes her strategy for reflection, reasoning, and analysis: "When I have an idea about something, and it differs from the way another person is thinking about it, I'll usually try to look at it from that person's point of view, see how they could say that's why they think that they're right, why it makes sense" (Belenky and others, 1986, p. 100).

She is playing what Elbow (1973) calls "the believing game." She enters into the argument by taking the other person's perspective. She tries to imagine how the other is thinking and what sort of sense the other is trying to make. Note, however, that her analysis is not blind acceptance. Like her separately thinking peer, she does not agree with the idea she is considering, but her way of approaching it includes an imagined relationship—or connection—with the author of the idea.

The third perspective for understanding the woman student's experience of the environment is her developmental position. There are five different epistemological positions from which women view the world: silence, received knowing, subjective knowing, procedural knowing, and constructed knowing (Belenky and others, 1986). In each one, salient meaning is made about the self, the nature of knowledge, and the nature both of authority and of being authoritative oneself. Each position describes a world view or framework for how the woman thinks about herself and how she experiences the contexts of her life. For an educator, understanding these positions provides not only another perspective for considering reentry women but also a perspective for considering one's own position as an adult.

From the position of silence, women experience themselves as mindless, voiceless, and completely powerless in relationships with whomever they perceive as authorities. As received knowers, they conceive of themselves as able to receive and reproduce knowledge from authority. Received knowers do not believe themselves capable of creating knowledge, nor do they imagine that creating knowledge is an aspect or value of becoming educated. As subjective knowers, women conceive of significant truth and knowledge as being privately constructed and subjectively known. Their assumption that this is true for everyone—themselves, peers, and authorities—leads to an interpersonal perspective that includes a certain measure of isolation from a community of peers or scholars. As procedural knowers, women are invested in learning and applying appropriate procedures for obtaining and communicating. Authorities are perceived as knowing how to do this, and they are valued for their capacity to teach it to others. Finally as constructed knowers, women see all knowledge as contextual and experience themselves and others as capable of creating knowledge. Since authority is divested of a certain amount of power, there is a possibility for collegial relationships to prosper (Belenky and others, 1986).

In summary, these three perspectives—voice, connected learning, and developmental position—can affect how we consider education for all students. The remainder of this chapter focuses on how these three perspectives provide ways to consider returning women students. As in Rita's case, the choice to pursue formal learning requires a woman to enter a new and often alien environment. Reentry may uncover issues having to do with social class (as it does for Rita), or, at the very least, it may mean reintroduction to an environment left years ago and may uncover old educational problems and issues. Regardless of her particular history, each returning woman student needs to develop a sense of her own power as a student and a knower, an understanding of and control over her approach to learning, and a set of realistic and articulated goals for what she wants to learn. These three perspectives help us explore how she makes meaning of this process. As educators or program designers, how well we understand her experience will profoundly affect what we provide, as well as such associated issues as retention rate and outcome measures.

Voice

One night, Rita is invited to a party at her mentor's home. We see her struggle with appearing appropriate, first by trying on a series of outfits, next by arriving at the party and then deciding she cannot go in. She leaves to join her husband and her mother at the local pub, having failed to get him to join her at the party. When she arrives, her husband, who scorn's Rita's desire to learn and the criticism of their life that her new goals imply, is happily singing songs. She slides in beside her mother, unable to join the singing. Rita understands her dilemma, and the pain of it is poignant. Later, she tells her mentor that her husband's intention had been to show off "some funny woman who thinks she can learn." Nevertheless, Rita has already gone too far to retreat. She explains that her husband "wonders where the girl he married went to," while she feels that her own voice in the family has seized up: "I can't talk with the people I live with." She begins to feel that the only place she can talk is in her mentor's office. In the pub, the singing had gone on, and tears fell slowly down Rita's mother's face as she turned to her daughter and said, "There must be better songs to sing." The film cuts back and forth between the pub scene and the mentor's office, visually conveying both Rita's transition between two lives and her conviction: "That's what I'm trying to do, sing a better song."

The metaphor of Rita's search for a "better song" captures the importance of her having and developing a voice as part of the project of educating herself. It is a common refrain among returning women. Sometimes it is expressed as a feeling of having been profoundly silenced or reduced, as a primary parent of young children, to "words of one syllable." Equally often, a student is aware that a distinctive aspect of her voice is missing. For example, the present author has been shown the following journal entry: "What I really need now is form—discipline, clarity, concrete knowledge in the areas in which I am lacking. I have been swimming in the waters of imagination for years now, and my strokes are pretty strong. What I need now is to come to shore and stand there, grounded and strong in real mental and physical capability. And I need improvement in verbal expression: technique, practice, mastery. With these tools, I will be able to expand." Comfortably acknowledging her need for "concrete knowledge," this thirty-eight-year-old woman ends her statement by emphasizing the importance of having and strengthening her voice so that she can communicate and "expand." Although she is confident of a particular knowing through imagination, it no longer feels discrete or integrated enough. Already strong in a well-developed "physical capability" to communicate (through dance), she yearns now to feel equally strong in "real mental capability"—in how she speaks and writes. She recognizes that until these capabilities are developed, she will feel constrained and ungrounded.

The capacity to engage in dialogue with others is perceived as a female-appropriate, nurturant, responsive style in relationships (Ruddick, 1980), yet in the "public" arena of the academic world (Martin, 1985), a woman quickly discovers that her use of voice is considered idiosyncratic. It is vulnerable to the judgment of being "too personal." She is told this in the margins of her early papers. She often hears the differences between how she frames a question and how others in the classroom speak. Her whole project of becoming educated begins to founder as she suspects herself of being somehow unfit. She is quick to understand these differences, because she has learned to be sensitive to explicit and implicit messages conveyed through dialogue. She may well conclude that, at the very least, she should remain silent until she can speak the language of the new culture.

This is a personally hazardous solution, since voice is a primary means and medium by which women develop relationships, and relationships are crucial to how women develop and monitor a sense of themselves and their identity (Baker-Miller, 1984). Thus, in contrast to earlier psychological theory, which posited identity development as a process of emerging autonomy, some current theory postulates that women experience themselves as developing a balanced identity grounded in interdependency with others. The adult learner finds herself in an environment where the very way she speaks is in question, and she begins to doubt that she has either a self or a mind: "When I included myself, sophisticated people rebuked me. I was told with annoyance and condescension, 'You always make it personal! You cannot argue abstractly.'

This happened often. I felt ignorant, stupid, female. And also confused. It seemed to me that the professors were talking somewhere in front of their faces, like the balloon in cartoon strips. Their talk seemed unreal, rootless, disconnected from themselves and consequently having nothing to do with anyone else either" (Rogers and Stevens, 1967, p. 202).

This silencing can have a profound effect. It does not just mean that the woman adopts a temporary silence; it often also throws her into a painful reassessment of her identity, her worth, and her abilities. A primary method for interacting with the world, and for adapting her self-concept to what she learns in those interactions, seems inappropriate and dysfunctional. A returning woman student may end her first semester feeling deeply shaken by this challenge and pervasively doubtful of her capacity to learn.

Some reentry women quickly understand that they are being challenged to develop a new voice. They may describe the process as an act of translation: learning to say, in academic language, what they already know or mean. They find themselves choosing to ask questions, risking the fear that the questions may make them seem stupid. In explaining what is involved in this act of courage, women often expand on a tenacious conviction that their life experience is relevant and frequently richer than that of their younger counterparts. A younger student may feel that developing her voice in the academy means a loss of her more personal voice. Returning women tend to describe this process as the task of gaining a new voice, although their other voices are less likely to be lost, especially if these women have the support of significant others in pursuing new endeavors. An experience of multiple voices may reduce the tendency to feel entirely silenced, but the issue of gaining the new voice is still crucial to returning women's experience of the educational environment.

Being heard, feeling herself a participant in good dialogue, and feeling that she can talk about her ideas—these are all essential to the returning woman if she is to develop confidence. Being heard is also intimately interwoven with her sense of herself as an informed and smart (rather than ignorant and dumb) learner. Frequently, the educational institution that she enters does not understand, respect, or find opportunities to support her effort. She grows acutely aware that all her conversations seem unreal, and that she has been cut adrift from significant ways to make meaning. She feels disconnected, isolated, and often scared. The experience of disconnection can be what is most disturbing.

Connected Learning

On the whole, our environments for learning have encouraged and rewarded the "separate" thinkers. Regardless of their gender, they offer a genuine sense of efficacy and power as they come to know the procedures of their disciplines and feel confident in their capacity to argue, write papers that are approved of, and think their way through complicated notions. In contrast, the connected learner's experience that her voice is inappropriate fosters a suspicion that her thinking process is equally unfit in the majority educational culture. While she is focusing on making connections, others seem to be looking elsewhere.

Throughout her adult life, she has tuned herself to her relationships as a way to orient herself to her world. Now, suffering double jeopardy as connected knower and adult, she is acutely sensitive to environmental cues from peers and teachers. She may find it difficult to ferret out the sorts of relationships she feels she needs. If she is in a classroom with primarily younger students, she is often aware that her energy for academic work seems to be more available than theirs. She may be concerned about who will babysit while she attends class, but younger students' concerns with social life, separating from parents, and being on their own for the first time are what fill their minds. The reentry woman suspects that the younger students resent her, either because her energy for studying (and the possibility that she is taking fewer courses) means that her performance may skew the grading curve or because they are still raging at their mothers, whose generation she represents. She may find that she is welcomed as a wiser woman by the younger ones, but this may leave her feeling reassigned to a mothering role when she is trying to explore other possibilities for herself. The very context in which she is hoping to learn feels fraught with complications. She feels, as Rita said, like "some funny woman who thinks she can learn." Adult students report feeling isolated and stunned by their loss of self-esteem: "I thought I knew something. Now I feel like I'm just trying to hold on to feeling like I'm worth anything at all."

Partly in response to this assault on self-esteem, and partly as a cognitive strategy, the connected learner tends to emphasize another relationship: the connection between her learning and her life. The returning adult is "experience rich, and theory poor" (Greenberg, Bergquist, and O'Donnell, 1980), while the reverse is true for the younger student. Thus, the returning woman often feels as if her learning is shaped by her making connections between what she already knows experientially and whatever the content of the course is. As one woman has reflected, "I don't know that I'm learning so much new, but . . . I'm organizing things, putting a name on them, and they are all falling into place for me." Another has summarized the process succinctly as "learning backwards," capturing her sense that as she learns new material, it refers her back to making meaning of previous life experiences. Freire (Green, 1975) defines this kind of learning as a significant part of the process of becoming a liberated and learned adult. It is the necessary codifying of background awareness as a basis of achieving new perceptions. On the whole, neither curricular structure nor teaching methods value this form of making meaning as a requisite part of learning; it is too personal. Further, in classroom discussions, women often join the dialogue starting with long stories that detail what seems relevant from their lives. They ground their learning and understanding in their experience, while the listeners, students and instructors alike, squirm. Unable to hear the logic of connection, and therefore the essence of the idea, the listeners are simply mortified by an apparently inappropriate sharing of life experience. They roll their eyes, the instructor tries to figure out how to break in, and the speaker begins to perceive that her presentation of the ideas, as well as the way she thinks about them, are wrong.

The learner often feels pervasively insecure about how she thinks. To address this deficit, she may well focus her attention on another relationship, the one with her teachers. Many adult women talk about how important it is to feel trust in a mentor or an instructor: to trust that he or she know what is important to learn, trust that he or she cares about students, and trust that he or she can teach them, even if he or she is younger.

To many faculty, trust seems a rather odd description of the nature of the relationship. The connected learner experiences an instructor by trying to take his or her perspective. Given the adult learner's sense of the relevance of experience to her knowledge, she wonders about the instructor's life experience. Meanwhile, as faculty, almost all of us have been well schooled in separating our lives from our teaching. Thus it is surprising, if not deeply disquieting, to discern that a student appears to be using criteria to evaluate us that feel strangely personal, even intrusive. The interpersonal dynamics that flow from this relationship are complex, often troubling, and sometimes exhilaratingly collegial (Daloz, 1986).

Still, as continuing educators, it behooves us to note that the relationship between adult students and their instructors is confusing and significant enough to have constituted the chief plot of several current literary dramatizations of adult learners (for example, *Educating Rita*). In these works, the woman student struggles to trust her male mentor as she moves through a developmental process of seeing him as brilliant, attractive, unreasonable, confused, and finally as an important intellectual colleague who must be abandoned if she is to develop her own sense of herself as a knower. Nor does the teacher have an easy time. His confusions mirror the student's as the relationship develops. Caught in a complex web of interpersonal issues, the instructor's responses vary. He is alternately an authority, a seductive peer, and an uneasy mentor. He feels pride in his student's accomplishment, as well as the pain of an abandoned lover. The woman student's relational and connected style may mean the uncovering of interpersonal issues that are usually inchoate in the academy. Moreover, since current statistics reflect the likelihood that the woman's mentoring relationship will be with a male faculty member, the further complexities of male-female relationships must be considered.

Overall, being in the academy and paying attention to relationships can have severe ramifications for the returning woman's self-perception and development as a learner. Feeling weird and inappropriate in relationships usually overwhelms one's capacity for increasing self-conscious evaluation.

Theory about educating adults emphasizes the crucial importance of adults' developing accurate perceptions of themselves and of their learning if they are to become effective lifelong learners (Brookfield, 1986). Most returning women students are practiced connected learners. Therefore, the kinds of experiences they have are very liable to make them foreclose on the process of self-reflection and to conclude that they are inept, not just different.

The present author's observations of women learners' development over time suggest that the learner's first sense of herself is fraught with doubt. After a year or two in a program, women retrospectively describe realizing that they had abandoned their own ways of thinking in order to fit into the new culture. Rita and her mentor, Frank, argue about this issue. Frank refuses to tell Rita how to analyze in preparation for a big exam. After having consistently critiqued her analyses for being inadequate to the ultimate goal, the exam, he expresses his worry that teaching her the proper forms for analysis will ruin her uniqueness. Rita is not interested, now, in being unique. She is interested in being one of the educated students. Yet, as we watch this interaction, we are aware that Rita may well lose the freshness of her insights.

Connected learners must learn to achieve a balance between connected and separate thinking. The latter frequently allows them to feel empowered; the attempt to find the balance helps them become conscious of how they learn. As one student describes the process, "I begin with my intuitive understanding. Then I read until I find my ideas confirmed, and until I feel like I understand the important conversations in the field." This description of reviewing the literature and synthesizing the primary arguments describes an approach to the task that is at once self-reflective and connected. There is an odd conundrum here: In becoming self-reflective, she has separated from herself enough to analyze her learning while still staying close to her own connected way of going about her education. Similar stories are related by students who assess their life experiences for college credit. What is important is that the learner finds ways to feel supported enough by the learning task before her that she begins to perceive how she is going about it and to abandon her image of herself as unfit.

Pedagogical and curricular strategies can support the connected learner in becoming self-reflective. These strategies appreciate her approach to learning. Journals, and reaction papers to reading, invite the connected learner into a relationship with course content that often feels appropriate, while the instructor's response to her writing supports her need for dialogue. Women's studies and black studies are often curricula in which students' experience is considered inextricably related to their understanding of the material (Maher, 1985). Collaborative teaching strategies, in which understanding and knowledge are defined as acts of social construction (Bruffee, 1986), also recognize that what is learned is inseparable from the process of learning. These approaches are models for organizing learning. They are also especially supportive of connected learners. Still, for the most part, these approaches to pedagogy and curriculum are considered peripheral to the majority culture of the academy, mere "add-ons" to its "real" programs.

Thus, recognition and support of the connected thinker's uniqueness, as well as the act of helping her in the process of articulation, self-reflection, and translation, define a relatively new arena for educational practice, not only with returning women but with all students. The ability of educators to address these issues has important implications for how well instructors can support learners to believe in their own capacities as thinkers and maintain that belief throughout their lives.

Developmental Position

The perspective of developmental position can sensitize educators to important distinctions among students. As Perry (1970) points out, once such sensitivity is developed, the instructor realizes that no matter what he or she teaches, the "appalling fact" is that the material and the teacher's role are perceived differently by each learner. Further, since instructors are also adults, their understanding and communication of the material, as well as the purposes of their instruction, are also likely to reflect epistemological distinctions related to their own developmental positions.

The details of developmental position describe possible perspectives that can influence learning, pedagogy, and the conceptualization and design of programs. For example, the received knower assumes that knowledge is delivered by authorities and that excellence is determined by how much learning one can reproduce. Returning women students who have this perspective frequently want clearly delineated programs. They assume that the ingestion of a required sequence of courses ensures that they will be educated and successful in their intended careers. As educators, we often conceptualize programs and curricula in the same way, developing course sequences that we assume will produce good managers or teachers, and so on. Similarly, the assumption that a learner is ready and able to participate in the collaborative construction of knowledge often undergirds designs for independent learning, whereas students' developmental positions may not be suited to such collaboration. Thus, the perspective of developmental position implies the need for a set of variables that can analyze assumptions about learners and about the process of learning. There are other implications for this perspective, specifically as it relates to the returning woman student. She may call on different perspectives in different arenas of her life. For example, she may experience her identity primarily from the perspective of one position, while she experiences relationships from another (Tarule, 1978). In teaching the perspective of developmental position to adult students, this theory of variance always emerges spontaneously in the discussion. Further, students expand the notion with the observation that they have differentiated ways of perceiving the disciplines themselves. As one student has observed, she knows that her understanding of math and science reflects received knowing, although in other disciplines she is aware that her thinking is more complex. Understanding these distinctions can create new ways to develop successful curricula and pedagogy in particular disciplines (Buerk, 1985).

The returning woman may also cope with the stress of the new environment by recalling and replicating how she was when she left college before, even if it was twenty years ago. Often she comes to the campus committed to finishing the degree she started back then, deaf to her own sense that her interests since then have changed dramatically. Even if she knows her interests are different, her sense of herself as a student may still be grounded in that earlier experience. The returning adult woman may be severely jeopardized in her first semester if she takes a course in the field she hated most as a young undergraduate, to prove to herself that this time she can do it better. Sometimes she can, but sometimes she feels that she has simply uncovered all the resistance she felt earlier. She may feel that she has regressed. If she is measured for epistemological level during the reentry semester, her apparent developmental regression may well be supported empirically (Griffith, 1980).

Both the variance within an individual's experience and the possibility of regression suggest possible areas for further research about developmental positions and about using the developmental paradigm as a theoretical basis for informing and expanding how to understand the special needs of returning women students. These suggestions are speculative, because developmental assumptions usually include the notion that the positions are hierarchical, sequential, and invariant. Nevertheless, those criteria are largely based on longitudinal samples of younger, traditional-aged students. Longitudinal data on adult students generally, and on returning women specifically, are still relatively sparse. More work will enrich not only our practice but also developmental theory as a whole.

Although the absence of longitudinal data limits this next idea to conjecture, a final speculation about the influence of developmental theory on the understanding of adults can be ventured. The developmental sequence of positions can be understood as describing two progressions: first, the unfolding over time of organized frameworks that define the limits and possibilities of a given individual's world view; and, second, the process by which new learning, and adaptation to new environments, proceeds in a much shorter time frame. With the latter perspective, returning women often describe their reentry and their learning in terms that echo experience of each of the developmental positions as they learn new material and a new environment. Hearing stories of a first semester, the listener hears students describing themselves as moving through the developmental positions. They talk about trying simply to understand the culture and the course content by receiving information and being told what to do. By the end of the semester, they may well have questions about their studies, and they feel confident that they are ready to join the conversation in their disciplines.

Whether students' evolution is over a long or a short time, instructors, once tuned to the positions as world views, can begin to hear about and evaluate students' progress in new ways. In a self-evaluative summary (Seawell, 1988), one woman captured the positions succinctly as she retrospectively described her experience. At first, she said, she could "pull off being a straight A student because the stuff that they wanted was just stupid . . . diddley facts and stuff." She began to realize, however, that she could satisfy her "curiosity" through studying, although she still found it hard to ask questions in class, "where you're made to feel like . . . something's wrong with you for asking." She recalled that, when she was younger, her father made her "feel stupid" for asking a question "just because of the way he'd answer it." She experienced him as "so much in the abstract that I couldn't understand." She "developed reticence" and began "reading, reading, reading," in which she "did not have to ask another human being." Quickly, however, she located others who cared about the same things, and "the whole process of dialogue opened up more and more possibilities for me." For her, the act of constucting knowledge came to depend on those dialogues, on "that kind of human interaction where you really can struggle with ideas, can share ideas, can without judgment look at things. Without that, the whole process of learning is empty" (Seawell, 1988). This student quickly traversed adaption to the educational environment as a received knower, withdrawing into her own subjective experience while she silenced her questions, and reemerging in dialogue about both the procedures for understanding and the collaborative act of creating knowledge. Her story reiterates the salience of finding a voice, connection with others in learning, and developmental position as a framework for making meaning.

She summarized how the three perspectives discussed here provide a way to consider crucial aspects in returning women's experience of our institutions and educational purposes.

Conclusion

In this chapter, the focus has been inside the returning woman's head: her experience of herself in terms of developing a sense of voice, creating connections through elaborating relationships, and conceptualizing her approach to the academy and to the material she is learning. The emphasis is on the learner's experience. As she gains a voice, she gains confidence in herself as a knower with a capacity to articulate and discuss her ideas. As she is confirmed and understands herself as a connected learner, she is validated and supported to become a lifelong learner capable of monitoring her own learning needs and procedures. Finally, epistemologically, she develops increasingly complex ways to think to understand.

These perspectives on students' experience can provide educators with lenses for viewing outcomes, shaping curricula and programs, and assessing the effects our efforts have on our students' development. Central to including these perspectives in educational efforts is the recognition that, despite all our attempts, the majority culture of the academy is still insensitive to the special needs of adult women.

References

Baker-Miller, J. *The Development of Women's Sense of Self.* Wellesley, Mass.: The Stone Center Papers, 1984.

Belenky, M., Clinchy, B., Goldberger, N., and Tarule, J. *Women's Ways of Knowing: The Development of Self, Voice, and Mind.* New York: Basic Books, 1986.

Brookfield, S. *Understanding and Facilitating Adult Learning: A Comprehensive Analysis of Principles and Effective Practices.* San Francisco: Jossey-Bass, 1986.

Bruffee, K. "Social Construction, Language, and the Authority of Knowledge: A Bibliographical Essay." *College English,* 1986, *48,* 773-779.

Bryant, D. *Ella Price's Journal.* Berkeley, Calif.: Ata Press, 1982.

Buerk, D. "From Magic to Meaning: Changing the Learning of Mathematics." Paper presented at the Workshop on Teaching and Learning Mathematics, Davidson College, Davidson, N.C., June 1985.

Daloz, L. *Effective Teaching and Mentoring: Realizing the Transformational Power of Adult Learning Experiences.* San Francisco: Jossey-Bass, 1986.

Elbow, P. *Writing Without Teachers.* London: Oxford University Press, 1973.

Gilligan, C. *In a Different Voice.* Cambridge, Mass.: Harvard University Press, 1982.

Green, M. "Curriculum and Consciousness." In W. Pinar (ed.), *Curriculum Theorizing.* Berkeley, Calif.: McCutchan, 1975.

Greenberg, E., Bergquist, W., and O'Donnell, K. (eds.), *Educating Learners of All Ages.* New Directions for Higher Education, no. 29. San Francisco: Jossey-Bass, 1980.

Griffith, J. "An Interactionist Elaboration of the Perry Scheme of Epistemological Development." Unpublished doctoral dissertation, Syracuse University, 1980.

Hall, R., and Sandler, B. *The Classroom Climate: A Chilly One for Women.* Washington, D.C.: The Project on the Status of Women in Education, 1982.

Kramarae, C. *Women and Men Speaking.* Rowley, Mass.: Newbury House Publishers, 1981.

Maher, F. "Pedagogy for a Gender-Balanced Curriculum." *Journal of Thought,* 1985, *20* (3), 48-64.

Martin, J. R. *Reclaiming a Conversation: The Ideal of the Educated Woman.* New Haven, Conn.: Yale University Press, 1985.

Perry, W. *Forms of Intellectual and Ethical Development of the College Years.* New York: Holt, Rinehart & Winston, 1970.

Rogers, C., and Stevens, B. *Person to Person: The Problem of Being Human.* Moab, Utah: Real People Press, 1967.

Ruddick, S. "Maternal Thinking." *Feminist Studies,* 1980, *6,* 70-96.

Seawell, M. "L: An Interview." Paper for Human Development Across the Lifespan course, Lesley College, 1988.

Shaw, G. B. *Selected Plays.* New York: Dodd, Mead, 1981.

Tarule, J. M. "Patterns of Developmental Transition in Adulthood: An Examination of the Relationship Between Ego Development Stage Variation and Gendlin's Experiencing Levels." Unpublished doctoral dissertation, Harvard University, 1978.

Jill Mattuck Tarule is a professor in the Counseling Psychology Division at the Lesley College Graduate School. She is also codirector of the Lesley College Project on Collaborative Learning. She has directed and been a faculty member in programs for returning adults at both Lesley College and Goddard College.

Higher education offers a plethora of programs and services for reentry women. Throughout the country, institutions large and small are finding ways to meet the needs of this special population.

Returning Women on Campus: Higher Education Takes Notice

Barbara A. Copland

That women are returning in droves to campuses throughout the nation is a truism in the late 1980s. In fact, the movement of reentry women into higher education has been in full swing for nearly two decades and shows no signs of abating. This chapter focuses on ways in which postsecondary institutions have responded to this population (by developing innovative programs, services, and practices to attract, accommodate, and retain reentry women) and provides a guide for institutions seeking to better accommodate this population.

A safe assertion about programs in higher education for returning women is that they are as heterogeneous as the population itself. As returning women defy neat classification, so do programs and services designed to ease their transition. The research on returning women, however, suggests a number of programs and services that should be considered in serving reentry women.

Scott (1980), in an exhaustive review of studies of returning women students, identified this population's characteristics, reasons for returning, obstacles and barriers, and needs, as well as the implications of this knowledge for practice. Among the suggestions are ideas about special programming, recruitment and orientation, childcare services, and career and academic counseling. Examples of these programs are highlighted in this chapter. Moore (1985) identified barriers that nontraditional female freshmen encounter as they seek entrance to four-year colleges and universities. Moore recommends that institutions actively recruit these women, provide orientation and seminars dealing with the issues of reentry, provide staff and peer counseling, and rid themselves of any institutional bias against nontraditional students. Suggestions for dealing with these issues are also included in this chapter. The present author's research on returning adult commuter students (Copland-Wood, 1986) will also be elaborated on.

In an effort to better identify what colleges and universities are doing to assist reentry women, the present author conducted a survey of forty-eight public, private, and two- and four-year institutions (Copland, 1987a). A survey (Copland, 1987b) was used to gather information on total enrollment, number of adult students, and administrative unit(s) that delivered programs and services for reentry students. The survey listed potential services, asked respondent institutions to indicate whether they provided those services, and, if not, whether they would like to provide them. The responses to the survey are the basis of this chapter.

While this discussion does not purport to be exhaustive on the subject of programs and services for reentry women in higher education, it does provide a comprehensive overview of what is available nationally to support the needs of this ever-growing population. By assessing what is, it is possible to formulate models of good practice while identifying exemplary programs that serve as models for other institutions.

Academic Programs for Returning Women

Academic programs for returning women, the very heart of the higher education enterprise, show a surprising variety. From weekend colleges and extended degree programs to competency-based curricula, colleges and universities are offering nontraditional academic programs to fit the schedules of reentry women who are employed or have heavy family responsibilities. Table 1 illustrates the scope of these offerings. For example, Alverno College (Milwaukee), a liberal arts college for women, has a weekend college; over half its students are twenty-five or older (Lewis, 1988). Students receive no grades, but they must pass course-content exams to receive credit. Chatham College's Gateway Program for nontraditional women offers degree and nondegree options. For degree students, a wide variety of internships and tutorials is available to enhance practical experience. Edinboro University's Opportunity College is primarily a delivery system to assist reentry women who have household or

Table 1. Nontraditional Academic Programs
at Selected Colleges and Universities

Institution	Program Title	Special Features
Alverno College (Wisconsin)	Weekend College	Pass/fail; no grades
Chatham College (Pennsylvania)	Gateway Program	Internships and tutorials
Edinboro University (Pennsylvania)	Opportunity College	Day, evening, and weekend courses
Hood College (Maryland)	Preview Privilege	Six weeks to take course for credit
University of Lowell (Massachusetts)	Second Chance	Open admission; first 30 credits
Mercyhurst College (Pennsylvania)	Adult College	Lower tuition; variable length sessions
Stephens College (Missouri)	College Without Walls	Required interdisciplinary course
Western Washington University	Fairhaven College	Self-designed degrees; no traditional exams or grades

employment obligations to fit degree study into their schedules. Hood College, in Maryland, offers the Preview Privilege Program which permits nontraditional students up to six weeks to decide whether to take a course for credit. Second Chance, at the University of Lowell (Burke, 1987), is a reentry program for nontraditional students who wish to study part-time during the day. It also provides support services, such as orientation and an adult drop-in center. Mercyhurst's Adult College is a special-delivery mechanism for reentry students wishing to study part-time. Sessions last from five to fourteen weeks. The College Without Walls at Stephens College (Littrell, 1986) is an academic program for reentry adults seeking the baccalaureate. A two- or three-week seminar forms the basis of this program, beginning with a three credit interdisciplinary course and including self-assessment, learning skills, advising, and degree planning. Finally, Fairhaven College of Western Washington University (Lewis, 1988) offers a liberal arts program in which students can design their own degrees. The program has no traditional exams or grades; assessments are conducted by students and faculty.

These are but a few of the special academic programs for reentry women. The variety is great, and the permutations are endless. Many of these provide specialized services to help ease the transition or reentry women into the college environment.

Table 2. Adult-Services Model Programs at Selected Institutions

Institution	Service Unit Name	Special Features
University of Illinois (Urbana-Champaign)	Office of Women's Resources and Services	Library on women's concerns; women's resource directory
University of Maryland (College Park)	Second Wind	Peer support; program handbook for reentry women; Warmline
Pennsylvania State University (University Park)	Returning Adult Student Center	Orientation; student organization; Outstanding Adult Student Award
University of South Carolina (Columbia)	Mature Students Program	Freshman core courses; incentive scholarship
University of Texas	Office of the Dean of Students	Returning student survival kit; childcare association

Adult-Services Model Programs

Table 2 provides an overview of five model programs that offer special services to reentry students. One program (University of Illinois) provides services through the Office of Women's Resources and Services. Returning women obtain information, general counseling, and referrals. Also available are a women's resource directory, (containing information about sources of assistance, both on and off campus), scholarships for women, the Illini Symposia for Women (all programs geared to women on campus), and a library of materials on issues of concern to women.

The Second Wind program at the University of Maryland is one of the oldest programs for returning women (Greenfeig and Goldberg, 1984). Initiated in 1976, it provides a low-cost, student-operated program of peer support, counseling, and advising. The Warmline is a telephone service whereby reentry students can get information and support during transition. An annual handbook of campus and community programs for reentry women, and a newsletter to sensitize faculty and staff, are two other components.

The Returning Adult Student Center at Pennsylvania State University offers a variety of programs and services for reentry students. The center provides information and referral; general counseling; orientation activities; special programming, such as brown-bag lunches; study, lounge, and kitchen facilities; lockers for commuters; a monthly newsletter; a guidebook for nontraditional students; and special awards, such as the annual Outstanding Adult Student Award, along with various receptions to honor nontraditional students.

The Mature Students Program at the University of South Carolina is another interesting model. It provides reserved sections of freshman core courses for reentry students, a preentry interview session for each reentry student, special registration for the first two enrollment periods, and an incentive scholarship program for women with great financial need.

Finally, another approach is featured at the program for reentry students at the University of Texas at Austin. Through the Office of the Dean of Students, special programs and services are provided, including information and referral, orientation, a mentor program, a childcare association, a returning adult student survival kit, a time-management guide, and periodic newsletters.

Other colleges and universities also offer services to reentry students, including Northern Michigan University, the University of Georgia, Indiana University at Indianapolis, Southeast Missouri State, Illinois State, Indiana University of Pennsylvania, Nassau Community College, Bloomsburg University, the University of Tennessee at Chattanooga, the University of Alabama, and LaGuardia Community College. This list is not exhaustive; it is only a sampling of institutions that have specialized programs. While the emphases of such programs vary, they tend to include such common elements as general information and referral, counseling, advising, orientation, informal programming, and peer support. This suggests that there is a model that has been widely adopted throughout the country.

Programs for Reentry Women

The remainder of this chapter will highlight specific programs and services that have been implemented for returning women, including orientation, counseling, advising, childcare, support groups, informal workshops and seminars, housing, special awards or honors, and student organizations.

Orientation. Several institutions feature orientation panels with "seasoned veteran" adult students who know the ropes (and some of the loopholes). At Pennsylvania State University, the panels are the core of orientation each semester, and they are offered in day and evening sessions to fit the schedules of returning students. Often included in the orientation program is a combined reception with the Continuing Education Division, which enrolls part-time evening students. Other activities are panel presentations by student services personnel, and campus and library tours. Copies of a twelve-minute videotape explaining the services of the Returning Adult Student Center are made available to those who are unable to attend orientation.

At the University of Texas at Austin, before the start of each semester, a series of programs designed for nontraditional students is provided. Information presented at these programs covers registration, time management, and other topics. The guide for new students is sent to students a month before classes begin, along with the orientation schedule. Two of the three summer orientation programs have been modified to accommodate the special needs of returning adults.

The Mature Students Program at the University of South Carolina has a half-day orientation session that includes a panel presentation by upper-division adult students. Student affairs administrators give testimonials and discuss survival strategies for new returning students. Students are also given writing exams to ensure their proper placement in English classes. They receive materials about all student services on campus that are available to adult students. Special computer-assisted registration is provided in this program to eliminate the anxiety of regular registration.

Phillips, Daubman, and Wilmoth (1986) outlined a strategy called "network intervention," which forms the basis of an orientation for returning graduate students. By increasing the social interaction between new graduate students and faculty, anxiety and poor performance are decreased. Components of the network intervention program include letters welcoming all new graduate students, personal letters of welcome from current students that include information packets, a family orientation picnic held before registration, a faculty-student wine-and-cheese party, monthly faculty-student potluck dinners, provision of a reading room and lounge for graduate students, and a manual outlining the objectives and operation of the network orientation program.

Some institutions offer credit and noncredit courses to help orient returning women to college. Pennsylvania State University offers a three-credit reentry course that contains units on study skills, learning strategies, adults as learners, and support services, as well as general information about the university. It also provides an opportunity for adult students to get peer support from other students in the class. A seven-week noncredit course on study skills for returnees is also offered through the evening continuing education program.

Widener University in Pennsylvania also offers a three-credit course for reentry women. The course provides a nonthreatening learning environment that helps alleviate students' anxiety and contains instructional components to help new students refurbish their academic skills.

The University of Maryland has been offering a one-credit course for returning adult students since 1974 (Greenfeig and Goldberg, 1984). It is taught by a professional counselor and includes assistance in choosing a major, academic advising, career planning, and vocational testing. It covers reading and study skills, common concerns, campus resources, and time management. Grades are based on attendance, class participation, personal journals, and two class projects.

Counseling and Support. Two common components of programs and services for returning women are counseling and support. Many of the orientation activities mentioned earlier include these all-important ingredients.

In a study of the adaptation of university counseling centers to meet the needs of an older student body, Mardoyan, Alleman, and Cochran (1983) found that nontraditional students differ from traditional students in four areas: their reasons for attending, their stages of development, their perceptions of the college environment, and their view of the world of work. Traditional students see college attendance as a normal progression from high school, whereas older students view it as a means to make a career change or advance, to obtain greater life satisfaction, or to help themselves through a transition in their lives. Developmentally, younger students generally are dealing with intimacy, whereas older students may have resolved this issue but find it threatened by their return to school. Younger students view college as a continuation of high school, while older ones often feel out of place on campus. In terms of work, traditional students may have unrealistic expectations about the work world, while older students, having been there, have more realistic perceptions. These authors suggest that older students need weekend and evening counseling hours, telephone counseling sessions, and childcare options.

At Pennsylvania State University, counseling needs for nontraditional students are met through individual and group sessions. Three to four support groups for returning adults and graduate students meet weekly on a semester-long basis to discuss issues related to reentry. A "women only" therapy group is offered to those who want greater understanding of themselves and ways of relating more comfortably to others. The groups, no larger than fifteen women, are typically led by licensed psychologists or doctoral interns.

Georgia State University has support groups for midlife students reentering college (Levin, 1986). The intention of the groups is to explore the interaction between academic stresses and adult-development issues. The groups work on coping strategies to ease reentry, especially time management, stress management, and biofeedback techniques. Some of the developmental issues explored in the support groups are bodily decline, family, work, biological timetables, disparity between expectations and career achievements, the financial pressures of being "in between" two generations, and the shift to a "time left" perspective.

In a study of support groups as a means of helping reentry women cope with school demands and their other responsibilities, Jacobs and others (1983) found that support groups at the University of South Carolina helped women deal with these stresses. Women who experienced more stressful life events at the beginning of school had poorer adjustment by the end of the semester, yet social support did help them adjust. The groups, ten weeks in length, began with discussion and prioritization of the issues that members wished to consider. The major group formats included sharing of ideas, role playing, and giving and receiving of feedback. The five major areas of focus were assertiveness, time management, self-concept, clarification of social relations based on new roles, and study skills.

Childcare. The issue of childcare is one of the most pressing and obvious concerns of reentry women. Without childcare programs that meet their requirements and schedules, many women are liable to delay college reentry until their children are in school full-time. Fortunately, childcare is probably one of the fastest-growing services for reentry women, because more institutions are recognizing that the nontraditional student population will continue to grow, and that to recruit and retain this population, specialized services are necessary.

Several institutions have solved this problem creatively. At Pennsylvania State University's New Kensington campus, there is a childcare center in the main classroom building. A cooperative venture, the childcare center is run by parent volunteers who work in exchange for care of their own children. The one-room facility, equipped with toys, is a short-term service to be used while students are in class or participating in other academic pursuits. The childcare center is also used as an observation site for students learning about early childhood education. For parents who cannot always spare the time for volunteering, there is a nominal per-hour charge per child.

All twenty institutions in the City University of New York system have childcare centers supported by city and state funds, as do institutions in the Connecticut State University system (Daniels, 1988). Mills College (Oakland, California) has twenty-four apartments reserved for adult students, particularly for those who have children (Daniels, 1988).

The University of North Carolina at Asheville, in response to a population of whom 50 percent are older students, offers childcare at certain events (Hall and Jovacchini, 1984). For a creative parenting workshop, a childcare room with a graduate student in charge was provided to participants. Funds were obtained from the division of student affairs. An adult student organization, ENCORE, was formed, and the group was able to provide childcare for selected activities by using funds raised from student activities fees. The service was free to students and cost one dollar per hour for faculty and staff. The advice of those who organized childcare services in Asheville is to start out small by providing care at a few events, rather than offering a full-time service.

In the University of Wisconsin system, each of the thirteen institutions has developed some type of program to assist students with childcare. All of these are on-site services. Two of the institutions contract with independent providers. The main campus, at Madison, offers a variety of campus centers, as well as a childcare tuition-assistance program. Assistance, if awarded, is paid directly to the providers of the childcare service. Funds for the various centers come from a variety of sources, including nonallocatable segregated fees, user fees, and donations. User fees make up the largest amount of the operating budgets. The system's policy is that affordable, high-quality childcare should be made available to students, faculty, and staff.

Housing. A unique program, the Single Parent Project, is taking shape at Goddard College (Vermont). Realizing that single parents could attend college without jeopardizing their welfare and Medicaid benefits, college officials at Goddard converted unused space in dormitories to four-unit residence halls to accommodate single parents and their children. Begun in 1987, the project allows single mothers and their children to live in dormitory suites while the mothers pursue degrees and the children are cared for by a center on campus. Goddard contributes about $2,000 per student for tuition, while state and federal money and private grants cover the rest. Each two-bedroom suite contains a kitchenette and comes furnished with beds, desks, and dressers. Families share bathrooms. Single parents are required to contribute eight hours a week without pay to the college work-study program. Families are able to remain in their living quarters during winter and summer breaks. The project is now housing twelve students, but officials hope to double that number very soon.

Workshops, Seminars, and Special Services. At the University of Georgia, the Women's Opportunity Network (WON) was established to assist nontraditional women by providing support throughout the university community (Copas and Divinell, 1986). A survey of the needs of nontraditional women by WON revealed interest in such topics as legal and consumer rights of women, strategies for career development and advancement, and managerial skills for women. Programs provided by WON include a reception for nontraditional women and an orientation session. The organization also collects statistics on nontraditional women and disseminates them to the university's board of regents.

One programming area that is gaining momentum in colleges and universities is designed for displaced homemakers who return to college. Women in this subgroup of the reentry population—generally described as twenty-seven years old or older and previously employed primarily as homemakers, not as paid workers—have lost the financial support of those on whom they depended and are not eligible for public assistance (Swift, Mills, and Calvin, 1986). Their problems are compounded by their feelings of isolation and their lack of financial resources, childcare services, and study skills, as well as by their low employment.

At the University of Toledo's Center for Women, three programs were created to meet the needs of displaced homemakers (Swift, Mills, and Calvin, 1986). Project Succeed, begun in 1984, provides on-the-job training while women attend school. Special services include paid internship or permanent job placements, career planning sessions, academic coursework, and professional and personal development workshops. A second program offers back-to-school workshops in local libraries and churches. Special programs to increase self-confidence are the third part of the thrust to assist displaced homemakers. These programs include such topics as how to handle money, how to get what you want out of life, and women and the law.

Brown-bag lunches for reentry students at Pennsylvania State University include such topics as aging parents, addictive relationships, male stereotypes, procrastination, and returning to the workplace from the classroom.

Needless to say, workshops and seminars for reentry women run the gamut of possibilities. Irrespective of the topic, however, their purpose is to help reentry women deal with some of the burdens and anxieties placed on them when they return to school.

Awards and Honors. For the past two years, the Returning Adult Student Center at Pennsylvania State University has been recognizing outstanding adult students selected by a committee from campuswide nominations. Announcements of the competition are placed in the local and campus newspapers. Faculty, staff, and students are invited to nominate nontraditional students on the basis of difficulty of circumstances, variety of roles, innovative approaches to completing college, support of others returning to school, contributions to the institution, efforts to sensitize the institution to the reentry student, grades, awards and honors, and statement of short- and long-term goals. The person selected for the award is presented a plaque at a reception in his or her honor. Local nominations are then made for a statewide competition.

Reentry women are often recipients of scholarships, *Who's Who* honors, and other campus awards, but this area appears to need more attention. Awards are not only a vehicle by which individuals can be recognized for their achievements, but also a mechanism for identifying role models for others facing similar challenges.

Student Organizations. The names given to many reentry student groups on various campuses reflect a sense of humor and pride in the experience of being an older student. Some examples are the Top of the Hill Gang, Primetime Lions, ENCORE, TNT: Typical Non-Traditionals, SOTA: Students Older than Average, and ANTS: Association of Non-Traditional Students.

The major purpose of these organizations is to provide support, social outlets, and advocacy for reentry adults. Many of these organizations are supported through student activity fees. Some are plagued by lack of resources. They may lack student participation as well, because of the multiple roles reentry students must manage. Nevertheless, the presence of such an organization on campus demonstrates a commitment to serving the nontraditional adult and returning student.

Future Directions

The reader may discern from this chapter that institutions of higher education are indeed taking notice of reentry women. In the main, this is true, although there are wide disparities from one institution to another. Some colleges are doing a great deal; others are doing nothing. Askell (1982) defined three stages of institutional adaptation to reentry students. These stages serve as a convenient checklist for institutions interested in becoming more responsive to this population. He calls the first stage of adaptation the *laissez-faire stage,* in which simple barriers to adult students are removed (age requirement, parental consent forms). The institution itself does not change. There is no active recruitment, no special support, no faculty development. Second is the *separatist stage,* wherein adults are separated from the major student body and given specially developed programs, usually at special times and locations. Fees are generally not adjusted, and support services are weak. There is usually a separate faculty, there is limited or tightly controlled access to mainstream courses, and the administrators of adult programs generally have limited power. Askell dubs the third stage the *equity stage,* in which there is active recruitment of reentry adults. Other features are appropriate delivery systems; fully integrated curricula and faculty; provision of credit for prior learning; administrative services available by phone, by mail, and in the evenings and on weekends; and academic advising available when adults are on campus. When equity is achieved, senior policymakers are aware of adults on campus.

Askell's model is particularly useful in thinking about the circumstances of returning women students. It has several policy implications. Institutions should modify their mission statements to include a commitment to serving reentry students, as well as other nontraditional populations. The president and other central administrators must express this commitment to their various constituencies (including faculty, staff, students, and the wider community). Any long-range or strategic plan of the institution ought to address the needs of adult students, and not just those who are twenty-five to forty-five years old, but also those who are in preretirement and retirement. Officers in student services, admissions, registration, financial aid, career development, and counseling must adapt their programs and services to fit the needs of traditional and nontraditional students alike. Methods and the timing of programs and services ought to reflect the varied needs of students, no matter what their ages. Finally, the institution must address the disparity that may exist between its stated policies on admissions, transfer, and residency, and the reality of what is needed for satisfactory academic progress on the part of all its students.

This chapter has provided some ideas for making college and university campuses more hospitable to reentry women students by focusing on programs and services being offered at selected institutions. Higher education has made great strides in the past fifteen years, but much remains to be done in this area.

References

Askell, E. F. "Adapting the University to Adult Students: A Developmental Perspective." *OECC News*, Spring 1982, pp. 4-6.

Burke, J. "Second Chance: An Innovative Program for Adult Learners." *Journal of College Student Personnel*, 1987, 28 (5), 470-472.

Copas, E. M., and Divinell, P. L. "Women's Opportunity Network: An Entity for Initiating Programs and Services to Nontraditional Women Students." *Journal of the National Association of Women Deans, Administrators and Counselors*, 1986, 46 (1), 23-27.

Copland, B. A. "Compendium of Programs and Services for Returning Adult Students." Unpublished paper, Pennsylvania State University, 1987a.

Copland, B. A. "Survey of Programs and Services for Adult Students at Postsecondary Institutions." Unpublished survey instrument, Pennsylvania State University, 1987b.

Copland-Wood, B. A. "Older Commuter Students and the Collegiate Experience: Involved or Detached?" *Journal of Continuing Higher Education*, 1986, 34 (2), 27-31.

Daniels, L. A. "The Baby Boomers Change Courses." *New York Times*, January 3, 1988, EDUC pp. 16-18.

Greenfeig, B., and Goldberg, B. "Orienting Returning Adult Students." In M. L. Upcraft (ed.), *Orienting Students to College*. New Directions for Student Services, no. 25. San Francisco: Jossey-Bass, 1984.

Hall, L., and Jovacchini, E. "Child Care for Campus Events: Assisting Adult Students to Assimilate." *Journal of College Student Personnel*, 1984, 25 (5), 468-469.

Jacobs, S. B., Unger, D. G., Striegel-Moore, R., and Kimbrell, C. D. "Mature Students: Providing the Support They Need." *Journal of College Student Personnel*, 1983, 24 (4), 372-374.

Levin, E. L. "Support Group for Midlife Students Reentering College." *Journal of Student Personnel*, 1986, 27 (4), 371-372.

Lewis, J. S. "Meeting the Needs of Adult Undergraduates." *The New York Times*, January 3, 1988, EDUC pp. 19-20.

Littrell, D. P. "Lifelong Learning—Sunrise Again: Addressing the Needs of Returning Adult Students." Paper presented at annual meeting of AAACE, Hollywood, Fla.: October 1986. (ED 279 287)

Mardoyan, J. L., Alleman, E., and Cochran, J. R. "Adapting University Counseling Centers to Meet the Needs of an Older Student Body." *Journal of College Student Personnel*, 1983, 24 (2), 138-143.

Moore, W. "Barriers Non-Traditional Age Freshmen Women Encounter as They Seek Entrance to Four Year Colleges and Universities." Unpublished doctoral dissertation, University of Oregon, 1985. (ED 277 332)

Phillips, M., Daubman, K., and Wilmoth, D. "A Graduate Student Orientation Program." *Journal of College Student Personnel*, 1986, *27* (3), 280-281.

Scott, N. A. "Returning Women Students: A Review of Research and Descriptive Studies." *Journal of the National Association of Women Deans, Administrators and Counselors*, 1980, *31*.

Swift, J. S., Mills, D., and Calvin, C. "Special Programming for Displaced Homemakers." *Journal of the National Association of Women Deans, Administrators and Counselors*, 1986, *50* (1), 3-7.

Barbara A. Copland is director of the Returning Adult Student Center and affiliate assistant professor of adult education at Pennsylvania State University, University Park.

With over 50 percent of the workforce now female, the workplace is slowly adopting supportive work structures and benefit programs to make it more feasible for women to combine work and family.

Supporting Women's Reentry to the Workplace

Karen E. Watkins

Women have been reentering the workforce in ever-increasing numbers. This chapter offers a historical perspective on women's participation in the labor force in order to illuminate the changing needs of these women for support. Innovative programs supporting reentry are shown to be those that take the long view of corporate and social needs. Since women now make up the majority of the workforce, their needs in terms of childcare, social services, and retirement insurance must increasingly be met if business and industry are to retain these valuable employees. The L & N School and the Caregiver's Project of the state of New York are examples of innovative programs supporting reentry.

The Changing Demographic Imperative

New Women's Labor Force Participation Rates. The percentage of married women in the civilian labor force, as reported in U.S. Census data, was only 4.6 percent in 1890. Working women aged twenty-five to forty-four represented 15.1 percent of the female population. Overall, women represented 17 percent of the civilian labor force in 1890. Women were discouraged from working by employers who required them to live in, as in the case of domestic servants, or by employers' (and public) pressure to resign upon marriage (for example, teachers and nurses).

Low wages, intermittent work, and poor working conditions contributed to women's low representation in the labor market. Vicarious achievement was also the norm. Women were expected to feel a sense of success if their male family members, bosses, doctors, or students were successful (Applebaum, 1981).

Even in 1940, when wartime exigencies required women to move into manufacturing and other traditionally male jobs, the total of married working women was still only 13.8 percent. In 1950, workforce participation increased to 21.6 percent, and by 1979 it was 49.4 percent, by which time women represented 42.2 percent of the workforce. This expansion of the female workforce after 1950 was disproportionate, with women aged forty-five to sixty-four years representing the largest group. Rapid, large-scale advances in job opportunities in the postwar boom period contributed to the increasing participation of women in the workforce (Yohalem, 1980; Applebaum, 1981). Citing similar U.S. Bureau of Labor statistics, Kahne (1985) illustrates that this dramatic rise in workforce participation rates of women, especially older women, from 1952 to 1982 was accompanied by a parallel drop among men of 4 or 5 percentage points (aged sixteen to fifty-four) and 17 percent at ages fifty-five to sixty-four.

Using industry labor market projections, coupled with demographic data, Kahne notes that industry expansion for the 1990s will be in service occupations, those that now have disproportionately more women and older workers. This, coupled with the aging of the baby-boom generation, suggests the potential for even greater workforce participation by these populations. With the current gap in longevity between women and men, women will represent a higher ratio of the older adult population. Changes in retirement benefits and cost-of-living increases may make at least part-time work a necessity for this group (Yohalem, 1980).

Social Changes. Other changes since 1965 have affected the workforce participation rates of women. Passage of affirmative action legislation, increased public concern over women's rights, a rising inflation rate that led to the need for wives' income to maintain a prior standard of living, deferred childrearing patterns, and briefer stopout periods for childbirth have led to higher participation rates by women in the labor force and some lessening of occupational segregation (Applebaum, 1981).

Nevertheless, recession may have a dampening effect on this growth. During the Great Depression of the 1930s, married women were literally forced out of the labor market, either through termination of their employment or discriminatory hiring practices, with preference given to employment of male heads of households (Applebaum, 1981). These practices also forced women to remain in certain occupational sectors. The affirmative action legislation of the 1960s may prevent a resurgence of these practices, but since there is a growing desegregation of occupations, burgeoning growth among "female" occupations, and decline in the workforce participation rates of men—some proportion of which is due to unemployment in "male" occupations—it is not inconceivable that these concerns will reemerge when the economy worsens. The impact of layoffs is especially hard on blacks and women, hired only recently as part of an affirmative action mandate, when seniority is the retention criterion ("last hired, first fired").

Questions of women's unequal pay or of equal pay for jobs of comparable worth also affect this discussion. As early as the Industrial Revolution in England, women's wages were 60 percent of men's. This disparity continues unabated. Gilder (1986) suggests that the earnings gap may reflect choices women are making. Quoting a study by the Institute for Research on Poverty at the University of Wisconsin, which used a complex formula for defining a person's "earnings capacity" (age, location, education, experience, training, health, and discrimination for women), the study found that married men exploit 87 percent of their earnings capacity and married women only 38 percent. In contrast to the men, the more earning capacity women had, the less they used it. Women favored part-time work (41 versus 17 percent), self-employment (an increase from 6 percent to 32 percent from 1972 to 1982, with women now forming sole proprietorships at a faster rate than men), and work adjustment (women physicians were found to see 38 percent fewer patients per hour than men physicians, and women professors wrote fewer books and research papers than men professors). Gilder quotes a study that claimed that the earnings gap could be explained almost entirely by differences in the years of continuous service and consequent differences in experience and training. Women who continue full-time employment do maintain wages equivalent to those of their male counterparts. To Gilder, then, the pay differential is a matter of choice. Whether or not these interruptions are truly a matter of choice or familial necessity, it is women whose careers are interrupted; thus, women pay the price.

Economic Consequences of Career Interruption. A number of studies have attempted to determine just what price women have paid for these interruptions. Applebaum (1981) used the National Longitudinal Survey of Mature Women database of five thousand women who were thirty to forty-four years old in 1967. This group has been surveyed seven times, the last time in 1976, through mail, telephone, and personal interviews. Applebaum studied those who elected to leave the workforce for at least three years and those who stopped working for fewer than three years. She found that women with a more discontinuous work history, who had withdrawn for more protracted periods, were less likely to have the same wages or status in their jobs as those who stopped out for briefer periods. The residual wage gap between the two groups went from four cents per hour in 1972 to thirty-four cents per hour in 1976. Applebaum's study suggests that women do pay a large financial cost for these child-rearing stopouts. They may also be paying a long-term price in health. She notes a study from the mid-1960s, which found that wives with children worked in the home a minimum of thirty-six hours a week on the average, whether or not they worked outside the home, while husbands worked on the average eleven hours in the home, whether or not their wives worked outside.

In an effort to develop a mathematical model for predicting workforce reentry of women, Even (1987) supports the idea that career interruption partially explains the wage gap between the sexes. Even attempted to determine what factors predict whether a woman will return to work, and after how long. He found that women suffered greater wage depreciation if they had higher levels of education and experience; that women who worked longer into pregnancy were much more likely to stop out for shorter periods of time (probably because they would suffer the least wage deterioration and would have job-search costs, since it is expected that they will return to their previous employers); that the more children, the longer the stop out; and that educational level does not predict the duration of a woman's career interruption. Even also found that a woman's probability of returning to work falls very rapidly. In other words, if she does not return to work after the typical maternity leave of six to eight weeks, the likelihood of her early return to work quickly becomes remote. Even's model makes clear the costs to women of these career interruptions.

Women who return to work after several years find that the men and women they used to work with have received regular pay increases, promotions, and on-the-job training that have made them more valuable to their organizations, at the same time that the reentry woman's skills have grown rusty and outmoded. Programs that support reentry women must assist them in overcoming this disparity. Cultural norms supporting differentiated home responsibilities, wage disparities, and occupational segregation will have to be challenged before many women will find it cost-effective to return to work: "It is assumed that in the future, as in the past, women's family responsibilities will continue to influence their work roles. Their work situation can therefore only be understood in conjunction with the requirements of family life. It is because important changes are taking place, both in family life and at work, that the position of the older woman seeking employment requires special study at the present time" (Seear, 1971, p. 11).

Meeting the Special Needs of Displaced Homemakers

Although much of this discussion has focused on married women as the most dramatically increasing segment of the workforce, displaced homemakers—women suddenly widowed or divorced—make up a growing portion of the reentry population. Since 1970, the number of women heading households has grown by 84 percent (Hacker, 1986). Federal funding to provide training for displaced homemakers has been targeted primarily toward welfare recipients and low-income women, and training is typically for low-wage jobs. The legislation inaugurating this training, the Comprehensive Employment and Training Acts of 1962 and 1973 (CETA), demonstrated both a recognition that this growing group was at special risk and a belief that training for work would reduce social welfare costs. It was not until 1978 that CETA legislation was specifically targeted toward displaced homemakers (Yohalem, 1980). Legislation in the 1980s created the Job Training Partnership Act (JTPA), which, like its predecessors, provided training and vocational counseling to a variety of low-income groups, including women returning to work. Unlike previous legislation, in which costs far overran returns, current legislation called for oversight and involvement by councils made up of representatives from business and industry, who help identify high-demand jobs and assist in placing trainees. The legislation called for those providing the training to be paid on the basis of successful placement, which was defined as retention on a job paying four dollars or more per hour for six months. This plan increased the likelihood that government training costs would be retrieved through taxes on earnings and through welfare costs that would not have to be expended. These programs have met with varying success and have served only a small portion of the women seeking to reenter the labor market. The JPTA is a significant program for this discussion, because of its provision for involving private industry. It can be hoped that industry representatives have attained an increased awareness of the needs of returning women.

Who Are Current Reentrants? The actual number is not known, but among 621,000 unemployed women aged twenty-five to sixty-four in 1977, one-fourth had not been employed in the last ten years. More than three-fifths of the latter were over thirty-five, and about one-third were over forty. Of the total number, almost fifteen thousand were women over thirty-five who had never worked at all. Fewer than 4 percent of those out of the labor force in 1977 expressed no desire to work at any time. Thus, there was a total potential pool of reentrants of twenty-two million women. Linear extrapolations from current trends would find women's labor participation rates exceeding those of men by the late 1980s (Yohalem, 1980). Clearly, this is a significant population with special needs. Over 60 percent of displaced homemakers are earning below the lowest living standards.

The Reentry Process. Applebaum (1981) analyzed a number of factors to determine what, among the things women do to prepare themselves to return to work, will affect their wages and the status of their jobs. Education and training, irrespective of type, proved valuable in increasing both wages and status. Even training that women took at home with children, without any expectation of returning to work, enhanced their prospects. Moreover, the better the woman's last job, the better the job she will obtain on her return to work.

As these individuals contemplate returning to work, they will face discouraging odds. They must compete with younger men and women for jobs they would long since have outgrown had they stayed at work. Their social status while at home has often been a function of volunteer work and of their husbands' status (generally higher than that associated with the jobs for which women must now apply), and they may feel threatened by having to consider jobs their children would find demeaning (Seear, 1971). Given this mindset, vocational counseling is often greatly needed, yet rarely is it available in the workplace.

Workplace involvement in education and training programs for reentry women has been limited. To date, retraining in such high-demand occupations as nursing, apprenticeship training (largely unavailable to women in the United States, according to Yohalem, 1980), and on-the-job training have been the forms available to reentry women. Given the essential role this training plays in improving women's reentry prospects, it is unfortunate that business is not more actively involved. Retraining is largely conceived of as training an employee in a current position in the company for a new job, rather than retooling anyone with rusty, outmoded, or inappropriate skills for new corporate needs.

What companies are doing is providing alternative benefit plans and flexible scheduling options and experimenting with work-at-home plans. They are also making information and support groups available for parents, two-career couples, single parents, and employees providing care for the elderly.

Workplace Programs That Support Reentry Women

New Benefit Options. Benefit programs have been characterized as the corporate social welfare system (Kamerman and Kingston, 1982). Before the Great Depression, companies sought to retain employees through such benefits as housing, medical care, schools, recreation services, religious facilities, advice and counseling services, food and other goods, pension plans, and profit sharing. After the Depression, companies could no longer afford these extras, and the federal government became the provider of welfare services. After World War II, wage freezes and a number of legislative decisions led companies once again to use benefits in lieu of wage increases to attract and retain workers. Companies now have diverse, often cafeteria-style benefit plans, yet these plans serve only a few. Less than half of all employed workers receive health insurance, paid sick leave, and pension plans, while only slightly more than one-third of employed women have these benefits (Kamerman and Kingston, 1982).

As companies acknowledge that "women professionals are the future of the business, and unless we provide the mechanisms that allow women to participate, we may not keep them involved" ("How Companies Help," 1987), new benefit plans have been inaugurated. These include policies for expanded maternity leave, paternity leave, and modified paid personal or sick leave, which allows parents to use personal or sick leave to stay home with sick children or older frail adults. These policies make it more feasible for women with children to reenter the workplace. Expanded family medical coverage and company health-maintenance organizations also offer greater protection for reentry women with children.

Called the wave of the future, these approaches allow employees options in types and extent of coverage (Kamerman and Kingston, 1982). Some companies allow employees to elect greater coverage at their own expense through payroll deductions. Employees have been very positive about these plans. At one company, over 92 percent of employees changed their benefits from the standard package, indicating that most employees wanted something other than what they would have had prior to the new options. In another company single mothers chose more vacation time and more health and life insurance over retirement plans (Kamerman and Kingston, 1982). Such choices may have repercussions over the long term, but the ability to select benefits that assist with parental needs clearly eases the current situation. There is no evidence at this time that provision of these benefits has encouraged women to return to work, but there is little doubt that these flexible benefit programs are supportive of women's family responsibilities.

Childcare Benefits. Perhaps the most supportive and expensive services now offered are childcare services. These include the provision of vouchers toward childcare, subsidies for a number of slots in nearby childcare centers, information and referral services, and on-site childcare. In 1977, on-site childcare centers had been adopted by very few corporations (only 2 percent), and the high cost, both in startup and company subsidization, was one reason. Some parents are also concerned when getting to their workplaces involves a long commute for their children and takes the children away from neighborhood friends, who are more likely to be in neighborhood centers (Kamerman and Kingston, 1982). Around 2,500 companies provided some form of childcare aid in 1985, as compared to only 600 in 1982, while about 150 have on-site centers (Bernstein, 1986). On-site centers serve only a small percentage of a company's employees at any given time, which may also alienate non-user employees. Nevertheless, when organizations with such centers were surveyed, they listed childcare benefits as an asset in attracting employees. They also reported lower absenteeism, improved worker attitudes, favorable publicity generated by childcare centers, and lower turnover rates (U.S. Department of Labor, 1982). The Dependent Care Assistance Program of 1981 also provided a direct benefit to employees by treating childcare assistance in the form of an on-site center, direct payment to a childcare provider, or reimbursement to an employee as a tax-free benefit. Married women employees make up about five-sevenths of the users of childcare services (Magid, 1983).

The high cost of operating an on-site center has led many employers to seek alternative forms of assistance. The Bank of America provided initial funding and got other organizations involved in a project to train individuals to be childcare providers. The project led to the creation of 1,000 new slots. Dayton Hudson and First Bank System, in Minneapolis, supported a company called Chicken Soup, which cares for children when they are ill. The 3M Corporation gave money to a local YMCA so that it could expand its summer center hours to accommodate working parents with children home from school (Bernstein, 1986). What these strategies have in common with voucher systems and subsidies to nearby centers is the employer's indirect involvement on a financial basis only, while the private childcare organization assumes responsibility and liability for providing the service on a preferential basis to the funding organization's employees.

Lenient workplace norms are an inexpensive approach. U.S. Census data from 1982 showed that 7.3% of mothers in central cities cared for their young children while working full-time, as compared to 7.1 percent of those in the suburbs and 10.5 percent of those in nonmetropolitan areas. Depending on the age and mobility of the infants and the safety of the work environments, bringing children along to work is also an option. Prospect Associates, a small firm of thirty employees, established a childcare room that parents furnished with toys and games, so that employees could bring their children with them to work when schools were closed.

Other inexpensive options used by employers have included relaxing telephone policies, which ordinarily prohibit employees from receiving personal calls at work, and even establishing a routine work interruption for parents to call home and check on their children when school lets out. Allowing access for older children to company-sponsored childcare providers after school is also helpful.

Educational programs on disciplining children, balancing home and work, and two-career couples are low-cost approaches to supporting the needs of many reentry women. Stautberg (1987) reports that the Philadelphia Banks offer seminars on such topics as dealing with routine separations, parental guilt, and prevention of parental burnout.

Flextime and Job Sharing. Flextime is one way employers have rearranged the scheduling of work to accommodate the family needs of employees. In this approach, employees can vary their starting and ending times, getting in eight hours of work but starting anytime between 6:30 A.M. and 9:00 A.M. and ending eight hours later. Hewlett-Packard offers flextime on an "honor" basis, in which the employee may vary his or her workday at will (Stautberg, 1987). Research suggests that families are not necessarily able to spend more time together with flextime (Kamerman and Kingston, 1982), but little systematic study has been done. Flextime may be especially useful for running errands or for handling family business.

Job sharing is another innovative approach being used by some corporations, such as Steelcase, Inc. (Stautberg, 1987), to vary employees' schedules to help meet their family needs. In job sharing, two employees share the same job, with each one responsible for half of it. This approach differs from part-time work in that it is usually more stable, and the details of coordinating work and scheduling are often managed by the job-sharing employees. This arrangement can offer them much greater flexibility, while ensuring management continuity of work, with little need for oversight. The workers, more than half of whom are women with young children, have the advantage of holding part of a full-time job, with its salary, benefits, and longer-term prospects (Kamerman and Kingston, 1982).

Part-time employment remains the single largest form of flexible scheduling, with one-third of all women employees working part-time (Kamerman and Kingston, 1982). Most part-time work is low-paying and in low-level occupations. Benefits are rare and truncated. In 1982, women made up 70.7 percent of the nonagricultural part-time labor force, and 75 percent of them (as compared to 25 percent of male part-time workers) worked part-time by choice (Kahne, 1985). One trend is toward permanent part-time work, which has the advantage of flexible time but also offers greater long-term career mobility and stability (Kamerman and Kingston, 1982; Kahne, 1985).

Flexible Places. Work-at-home options have increased significantly (Pfeffer and Baron, in press), stimulated considerably by the development of the computer. Such work is often paid for on a piece-rate basis. Because these workers can choose when they produce each piece, maximum time flexibility is available for women with family responsibilities. There is also a greater possibility that women who are allowed to work at home after the birth of a child will reenter the workplace sooner, creating only a brief disruption in their contribution to their organizations. Overall, women in such "cottage industries" have received low pay, have been underemployed, and are not protected by labor laws limiting hours of employment and guaranteeing safe working conditions.

Creative Workplace Resources for Reentry Women

On-Site Childcare: The L & N School. Lomas and Nettleton, the largest independent mortgage broker in the world, designed its new Dallas service center, built in 1984, with an on-site childcare center, the L & N School, as an integral part. The center, which cares for 110 children aged six weeks to six years, is housed on the main floor, across from the cafeteria. Adults eating in the cafeteria, enjoy a view of children playing in their yard. During the last year, they have been entertained by an Easter parade, Fourth of July parade, an art fair, a Christmas concert (held in the cafeteria), and numerous daily reminders of the precious reasons for which many of them work. The center's director says that parents frequently visit their children on breaks, and nonparents often walk through the center to relax (Baldwin, 1987). Parents may eat with their children, come to nurse a child, come down if a child is unhappy or fretful, or share special moments. One father said, "Tomorrow my son is having a birthday party, so I will be down here. You can't put a value to this school system. . . . They could change a lot of things about my job that I wouldn't like, but I wouldn't leave this company" (Kennedy, 1986).

Why would a company like Lomas and Nettleton invest in an on-site center? Perhaps the kind of loyalty found in this parent's comment is one reason. A recent study at the company also showed a reduced absenteeism rate among center parents, as compared to all other employees. The company's senior vice-president of human resources believes that the center has also reduced turnover (Baldwin, 1987). Still, corporations are unlikely to invest in childcare, for financial reasons. On-site centers require the payment of hefty insurance premiums and almost always require corporate subsidization. To provide high-quality care at the L & N School, the corporate subsidy is between 50 and 60 percent. It was the vision of Mr. and Mrs. Jess Hay that led to the creation of the L & N School. Mr. Hay, who is the chief executive officer of Lomas and Nettleton, also serves as chair of the Dallas Childcare Partnership, a nonprofit advocacy organization for high-quality childcare. The Hay's dream is to create "the finest developmental school for young children." Hay says, "The nature and quality of our society 20, 40, 50 years from now will be tremendously influenced by the quality of child care available in our community" (Welin, 1986). In a recent news conference, Hay speculated that 90 percent of all preschool children may need childcare outside the home by the year 2000 (Welin, 1986).

The L & N School has received accreditation from the National Association for the Education of Young Children, which sets very stringent standards, and also from the mayor's childcare task force of Dallas. Quality, rather than cost, is clearly the hallmark of this center.

Center records do not indicate whether a parent is a woman returning to work, but eighty-two of the children's mothers are employed by Lomas and Nettleton, and eighteen of them have both parents employed by the company. Payment of childcare tuition is through a payroll deduction. Since children may begin coming to the center as young as six weeks, women are less likely to have significantly long career interruptions. For women reluctant to return to work because of concern for the quality of the care their children will receive, the presence of this nationally acclaimed, well-staffed, accessible, visible, on-site center should be reassuring. For those whose hiatus has been longer and whose children have grown, the corporation's visible commitment to the family needs of its employees may also help them feel more at home. The center sponsors lunchtime seminars on child-related issues and has a child-development library from which parents may check out books. The associate director facilitates three parental support groups, divided according to children's ages and stages. These educational activities also make the return-to-work transition much easier for women.

Many companies have nonprofit foundations through which they give large amounts to fulfill the dreams of owners and employees. College scholarships, matching gifts to an employee's alumnus, and grants for research for future product development have all been examples of ways companies give back to society and to their employees some measure of their profits. In-plant childcare is yet another way a company can help give employees not only current but also future support. If Jess Hay is right, childcare subsidies of many kinds may be necessary in order for many women to work at all, and companies can ill afford to lose so substantial a portion of the labor force. Yet the real issue will be whether companies will seriously commit the needed resources for high-quality of childcare. Without it, the impact on society and on the labor force in twenty years may be devastating.

The Elder Caregiver's Project. Children are not the only vulnerable family members for whom women have traditionally provided care. Through a grant from the state of New York, agencies and corporations are learning about the needs of those who provide care to infirm elders. Carol Nowak and Gary Brice, at the Multidisciplinary Center for the Study of Aging of the State University of New York, have been conducting this training project. Partial funding from the Travelers Insurance Company at Buffalo enabled Brice to do a thorough literature review and study of the impact of elder care on employees.

Caregiving is any type of helping activity other than providing financial support and may include such incidental tasks as doing chores, helping with personal care, giving injections, and doing such essential tasks as feeding an elderly person. According to Kahne (1985), 70 percent of caregivers are women. Results from Brice's study of caregivers in the

Buffalo office of Travelers Insurance were compared to a similar, large-scale study of the home office of Travelers Insurance. In both, caregiving led to significant disruption of the caregiving employee's work life, including more absenteeism, resignations, shifts to part-time work, long telephone calls during working hours, and lowered productivity due to stress (Brice, 1988).

With the aging of the baby-boom generation, increased longevity (especially of women), delayed childrearing, increasing female heads of households, and increased workforce participation by women, the conditions exist for a potential crisis in elder care. Returning women, generally between forty and fifty-five years old, now often have responsibility for both young children and older relatives. The original Travelers Insurance study found that 28 percent of the employees studied spent more than ten hours per week giving care to elderly relatives and friends, with 8 percent devoting thirty-five hours, or almost a second work week, to this task. They had been providing help for an average of five-and-a-half years, and 30 percent had not had a vacation from caregiving for more than a year. Among the elderly, 51 percent had two or more ailments, and only 3 percent had no medical problems (Collins, 1986). In a study of seventy-seven caregiving women (Gibeau, 1987), 77 percent of the women reported work and caregiving conflicts, 35 percent said their work was adversely affected, and 21 percent had considered quitting their jobs. Brice (1988) quotes one study in which two-thirds of the caregiving women had children under eighteen living at home, as well as the earlier Travelers Insurance study, in which 29 percent had children under the age of six. The stress on these women is enormous. Over the long term, career interruptions, enforced geographical stability, reductions in hours, and unpaid leaves will result in reduced medical and pension coverage for this generation of women caregivers. Added to the potential economic cost, women may also pay a serious health price in attempting to care for children, older relatives, homes, and careers simultaneously. In the Travelers study, some caregivers reported spending eighty hours beyond their full-time jobs in caregiving responsibilities (Collins, 1986).

Corporate support for elder care is still very tentative and consists primarily of education and information. Pepsico, IBM, and Southwestern Bell Telephone Company publish manuals for their employees to link them to local agencies. Travelers Insurance Corporation publishes resource materials on elder care. Remington Products, Inc., funds a respite program, which offers relief to caregivers through adult daycare, homecare, and institutional care.) Champion International Corporation offers a six-month unpaid family leave program. Intergenerational day care is provided by Stride Rite Corporation and by the Great Valley Corporate Center. The American Association of Retired Persons has developed a program kit titled "Caregivers in the Workplace" to help employers conduct caregiving surveys, hold caregiver's fairs, offer educational seminars for caregivers, and use a care-management guide to counsel employees ("Symposium on Aging," 1987). Other assistance needed by caregivers includes flextime (although Brice notes that this may not reduce the stress on caregivers, because elder care is often unpredictable and a reaction to crisis), the ability to add dependent elders to one's health insurance, support groups, and programs to prepare employees to think of their own and their parents' economic security and health (fitness programs, long-term care insurance, and so on).

Since many caregivers mask their problems and get others to cover for them, evidence of the toll that caregiving takes is often invisible until an employee is in trouble. Early-warning signs should be identified, such as frequent tardiness, absences, and long telephone calls. Once identified, caregiving employees should be referred to employee assistance counselors or agencies. Perhaps the single most important corporate response to the elder-care needs of employees will be to allow some time for employees to work out caregiving arrangements while also making the problem discussable. When family problems legitimately interfere with work, employers must decide whether to respond with compassion. Neglecting the needs of the caregivers of older adults has the potential of damaging corporate productivity by turning away many excellent workers at a time when the latent labor force is dwindling, while also devastating the social welfare of a large number of older adults.

Recommendations for Improving Workplace Responsiveness to Reentry Women

Corporate Self-Interest. Corporations are not developing programs to meet the needs of returning women. They are establishing such things as on-site childcare centers when they believe this will help them attract and hold highly qualified women workers. "Besides trying to make life easier for women workers, companies are concerned with the productivity lost when employees deal with family problems at work" (Bernstein, 1986). If companies are reluctantly allowing more part-time work, it is often because they want to keep particular employees, or because they save money in wages and benefits. They have sought to recapture childcare benefits in regained productivity. A study by Kanter (quoted in Gerber, 1987), based on twenty years of financial performance, found that companies with innovative human resource practices consistently outperformed nonprogressive companies in terms of sales, assets, return on equity, and return on total capital. Thus, there is evidence that providing more flexibility and increased benefit options will be cost-effective over the long term. From a social viewpoint, there is little doubt that corporations that take the fifty-year view of Lomas and Nettleton, or of an elder-caregiver benefit provider, will have the greatest impacts on long-term productivity.

Training, Retraining, and Apprenticeships. Women have had little success getting into apprenticeship training programs (Yohalem, 1980). Since women tend not to join unions and are underrepresented anyway in union-dominated professions, this superb form of retraining is often not an option for reentry women. One way to improve the success of these women will be to work to open up the union-financed apprenticeship programs to them. Apprenticeship training programs are particularly appropriate for reentry women because they often include some pay while training, offer on-the-job experiences, and include guaranteed placements. Jobs for which apprenticeship training is available also tend to be skilled jobs; hence, they are likely to be higher-paying. Union sponsorship also usually means that a number of other resources and supports are available, which can ease the transition process.

Retraining programs in corporations (unlike the JTPA, which is for reentry women) are for their own employees. By having access to spaces in retraining programs, reentry women could be retooled for new, existing positions in the company. Since JTPA assistance is usually geared to low-level occupations, corporate retraining programs would also give reentry women an opportunity to train for more skilled positions.

Corporate-sponsored educational programs that support a woman in all of her life phases and responsibilities have been emphasized here. Training may be about agencies available to help her deal with elderly dependents, or it may involve discussion groups on how to balance home and work, but educational programs that respond to family needs provide support and build morale for reentry women.

The Bottom Line. "A good support system is the single most important aid if a woman is to remain an effective employee" (Stautberg, 1987). As most women continue to enter the labor market out of economic necessity, their need for support will increase, while their ability to purchase support services on their own will decrease. Whether corporations play a significant role in helping to provide such support will ultimately be determined by their own self-interest. As corporations begin to acknowledge the intimate connections between corporate policy and family life, families may have to weigh their commitments to work and home differently. If American corporations were to adopt the social-welfare stance of Japanese corporations and guarantee lifetime employment, would families also make a corresponding commitment? Families might become intergenerational employees of a firm and might share the fate of the corporation by taking less pay when profits went down, more when they went up, and so on.

Changes in family structure and workforce participation by women are placing serious stresses on families, society, and the workplace.

Employers' responses may lead to very different policies. At present, many innovations in work scheduling and employee benefits suggest that corporations are struggling to respond to their changing workforces. Unfortunately, few of these enlightened benefits are available to blue-collar, low-paid women. Indeed, the options most readily available to them—part-time and temporary work—merely reinforce the conditions distancing them from these benefits. Since most returning women are in low-paying jobs, the present availability of services is almost nil for them (beyond the information, referral, counseling, and resource-giving services already mentioned). Perhaps the single most important agenda for corporations and government agencies will be to find ways to provide economically viable support to the low-paid returning woman employee. It will not be easy.

References

Applebaum, E. *Back to Work: Determinants of Women's Successful Re-entry*. Boston: Auburn House, 1981.
Baldwin, P. "Firms Turn Attention to Child Care." *Dallas Times Herald*, Sept. 20, 1987, pp. K-1, K-6.
Bernstein, A. "Business Starts Tailoring Itself to Suit Working Women." *Business Week*, Oct. 6, 1986, pp. 50-54.
Brice, G. "A Profile of The Travelers Insurance Company (Buffalo Office) Employee Caregivers to Older Adults." Unpublished draft report. Buffalo: State University of New York, 1988.
Collins, G. "Many in Work Force Care for Elderly Kin." *The New York Times*, Jan. 6, 1986, p. 5.
Even, W. "Career Interruptions Following Childbirth." *Journal of Labor Economics*, 1987, 5 (2), 255-277.
Geber, B. "Pushing for Part Time." *Training*, 1987, 24 (12), 59-66.
Gibeau, J. "Working Caregiver Survey." *Older Americans Report*, Dec. 4, 1987, p. 6.
Gilder, G. "Women in the Workforce." *The Atlantic*, Sept. 1986, pp. 20, 22, 24.
Hacker, A. "Women at Work." *The New York Review*, Aug. 14, 1986, pp. 26-32.
"How Companies Help." *Nation's Business*, May 7, 1987, p. 27.
Kahne, H. *Reconceiving Part-Time Work: New Perspectives for Older Workers and Women*. Totowa, N.J.: Rowman & Allenheld, 1985.
Kamerman, S., and Kingston, P. "Employer Responses to the Family Responsibilities of Employees." In S. Kamerman and C. Hayes (eds.), *Families That Work: Children in a Changing World*. Washington, D.C.: National Academy Press, 1982.
Kennedy, J. M. "Day Care Spreading in Industry." *Los Angeles Times*, Sept. 16, 1986, pp. 1, 18.
Magid, R. *Child Care Initiatives for Working Parents: Why Employers Get Involved*. New York: American Management Association, 1983.
Pfeffer, J., and Baron, J. "Taking the Workers Back Out: Recent Trends in the Structuring of Employment." In B. Staw and L. Cummings (eds.), *Research in Organizational Behavior*. Vol. 10. Greenwich, Conn.: JAI Press, in press.
Seear, B. N. *Reentry of Women to the Labour Market After an Interruption in Employment*. Paris: Organization for Economic Cooperation and Development, 1971.

Stautberg, S. "Status Report: The Corporation and Trends in Family Issues." *Human Resource Management*, 1987, *26* (2), 277-290.

"Symposium on Aging." *Elder Press*, Spring 1987, pp. 4-5.

U.S. Department of Labor. *Employers and Childcare: Establishing Services Through the Workplace.* Washington, D.C.: Women's Bureau, U.S. Department of Labor, 1982.

Welin, C. "Two Day-Care Centers Lauded for Quality Preschool Care." *Dallas Morning News*, Apr. 24, 1986, p. H-3.

Yohalem, A. "United States." In A. Yohalem (ed.), *Women Returning to Work: Policies and Progress in Five Countries.* Montclair, N.J.: Allenheld, Asmun & Co., 1980.

Karen E. Watkins is assistant professor of adult education and human resources development at the University of Texas at Austin. Her research and publications emphasize the promotion of sound human resources practices in a variety of settings.

Community-based organizations are in a unique position to offer client-focused basic education and training to returning women.

Community-Based Training for Reentry Women in Nontraditional Occupations

Ruth S. Howell, Helen Schwartz

Community-based organizations (CBOs) are very successful in training low-income and minority reentry women. Not only do CBOs equip women with the skills they need to get and keep jobs, but they also offer a highly supportive atmosphere within which women can begin to tackle all the questions, hesitations, and fears they face upon leaving the home to enter the labor market. By virtue of their close ties to their constituent communities, CBOs are able to offer uniquely adapted programming for returning women. They are experienced in coupling basic educational instruction with vocational skills training by combining flexible program design with a variety of support services.

Economically and educationally disadvantaged women, the populations that community-based organizations serve, need these support services to work through the multiple social and logistical barriers that prevent them from finding and keeping decent jobs. In fact, this need overrides their need for educational services, and any attempt to provide education without attention to special needs is doomed to failure.

This chapter describes the components that are integral to CBO programming for returning women, include recruiting, intake, teaching tech

L. H. Lewis (ed.). *Addressing the Needs of Returning Women.*
New Directions for Continuing Education, no. 39. San Francisco: Jossey-Bass, Fall 1988.   65

niques and strategies, placement and follow-up, while simultaneously focusing on the recruitment of reentry women to train for nontraditional occupations. Training in nontraditional fields not only affords women an opportunity to earn higher wages but also opens a new arena in which they can become highly competitive.

Recruitment

Recruiting reentry women for nontraditional skills training requires a special effort on the part of CBOs. Even though nontraditional jobs generally offer higher starting salaries, greater career mobility, and a special pride that comes from working for higher pay in more respected fields, many women are either unaware of these kinds of job opportunities or wary of working in predominantly male settings. They believe the myths that perpetuate the artificial division between men's work and women's work. The challenge for program recruiters is to help women overcome this ideological barrier so that they will consider nontraditional careers. CBOs can do this in several ways. Promotional materials need to be developed that expose the fallacies and debunk common myths by asking: Is women's work inherently different from men's work? Are women who work in men's jobs less feminine? Do women have the physical strength to do men's work? Is it true that women cannot understand the math and technical theory in men's work and will therefore never be competent to do men's jobs?

The role of program recruiters is to help women understand the range of nontraditional options that are available and how women's experiences and interests correspond to each option. Recruiters should personally convey to each woman that she can be successful in a nontraditional occupation, that many other women just like her have succeeded, and that many women working in nontraditional fields feel satisfied with their choices.

CBOs can plan recruitment campaigns that are focused on the target population. Community job fairs, adult remediation classes, preskills training programs, Head Start classes, displaced-homemaker programs, and vocational rehabilitation centers are prime sources for reaching highly motivated women who have committed themselves to self-improvement. While visiting with women attending these programs, CBO recruiters can distribute bilingual materials and respond to questions.

Help from counselors in other agencies that serve similar populations should be solicited in any recruitment campaign. Staff from housing projects, local welfare and unemployment offices, other CBOs, job training offices, parent-teacher associations, infants' and children's services, community centers, and neighborhood health clinics are referral sources for applicants. Another important resource is the clergy in the targeted communities. With ministers, as with all other contact people, it may be necessary to sell the concept of nontraditional jobs and skills training for women. Unless the clergy believe that the program offers viable job opportunities for women, they will not encourage their parishioners or friends to enroll.

An effective recruitment technique is an open house, preferably held at the training site. At open houses, staff members and program graduates can personally describe the typical career ladders and the logistics of the training program. Open houses that offer opportunities for hands-on experience are the most effective at convincing returning women they are capable of learning technical skills. A series of positive hands-on experiences can lead them to consider job fields they may never have envisioned for themselves. For example, Hartford College for Women and Hartford Area Training Center, both of which offer nontraditional skills training, developed a joint recruitment campaign. A large recruitment meeting was held, to which role models from the machining and cable television industries came wearing their uniforms and carrying their tools. They explained the daily work routines and why they liked their new jobs. The director of each program commented on his or her program, and staff from the funding source described the application process. A variety of career opportunities were discussed, and the women who attended responded positively to the session because it enabled them to obtain a truer understanding of the field.

In describing training programs, the entry requirements must be clearly stated in all program publicity. Brochures should also emphasize the ways in which programs offer special support to reentry women, such as academic and personal counseling, childcare and transportation assistance, refresher courses, mathematics review, physical-strengthening classes, effective-parenting classes, and so on. The language in all publicity must emphasize that women are welcome and that family members are encouraged to visit the program. While men typically assume that they are included in technical programs, women often assume that they are not. Consequently, they need special encouragement and support from their significant others in order to attend.

Some of the most effective recruiters are women graduates, because they can respond convincingly to applicants' fears by sharing personal success stories. They alone can convey their satisfaction with their nontraditional choices and can testify about what the programs and jobs have meant to them. The role of a recruiter is never to entice women into the program, but rather to offer the training as a viable option and to help them make informed choices.

Very aggressive follow-up of all contacts provides extra encouragement to women who might otherwise eliminate themselves before completing the application process. Follow-up mailings and telephone calls in response to each inquiry encourage women who are undecided or who need additional information. Occasionally, a second call to a woman who expresses ambivalence about the program or who misses an interview appointment can provide the added support that a returning female needs to make her decision.

Intake

The intake system of any nontraditional training program is critical, because significant numbers of women who make inquiries into nontraditional training will never go beyond the inquiry stage and become lost to the system.

From the first telephone call or visit, a welcoming supportive atmosphere must be established. One or two people should be designated to take all incoming calls about the program. If there is a bilingual component, the intake must be done in both languages. Intake workers should be trained to set a supportive tone while they inform prospective trainees about requirements.

In general, the requirements for CBOs that do training with Job Training Partnership Act (JTPA) funds can be very burdensome. Incoming clients are required to document personal information about themselves (for example, economic status, residence, and place of birth). In addition, each program has its own special requirements, such as a requisite level of reading or mathematics skills, as defined by the job and the job training. These levels are determined by testing. A woman who is receiving public assistance and who has been dealing extensively with the welfare system may find all the required paperwork and testing too burdensome. Therefore, it is important to provide the applicant with direct help and support as she wades through this bureaucratic sea of forms.

Intake testing must be administered in a supportive atmosphere. CBOs must take care that the screening instruments they select do not eliminate women or minorities on an artificial basis. While CBOs must screen for real job barriers (poor eyesight or hearing, insufficient language proficiency when no remedial instruction is available in the training program), they can also supply information that an intake worker can use as the basis of counseling. For example, if there is a need for higher math skills, how can the program help develop such competency? If a woman is lacking childcare or transportation, how can the staff help her make the necessary arrangements? The intake staff must make an overall commitment to recruiting nontraditional candidates into the program—not just those who have already learned the skills of the trade, but those who have the capacity and the motivation to develop skills during training.

Support Services. The provision of support services must begin with the intake process. A woman being plagued by bills, lacking transportation, facing a housing crisis, and dealing with inadequate or unreliable childcare is hardly in a position to enroll in a program successfully. These issues must be dealt with immediately, either by the staff or through referrals to appropriate agencies. All recipients of state assistance must be reminded of how their welfare grants are affected when they enroll in training or take jobs. They must understand the financial implications of their options.

It is also important to assess how a woman's spouse, partner, or family feel about her entrance into such an educational program. She may need special support and encouragement to overcome the negative pressures of a jealous spouse who is exerting pressure on her not to enroll. For example, in one bilingual class at Hartford Area Training Center's Precision Machining Training Program, a woman reported that her husband wanted her to leave class because he did not like her spending the day with so many men. The program staff invited the husband into the classroom with her for a few days to see what it was actually like. They also urged him to enter the program. Both interventions helped to defuse his antagonism and allowed her to remain in the program.

A number of CBO training programs are developing techniques for involving the whole family, or support systems composed of the women participants, at significant points throughout the training. To elicit support for their participation in the program, applicants and participants are encouraged to bring their spouses, partners, friends, and children to open houses and have them make regular class visits. Significant others might be asked to help develop plans with the individual participants for how household tasks will be redistributed during the months of training, or to help them practice training-related skills they need to develop. Each contact with the program helps significant others understand the women's participation and encourages recognition of their success.

Remediation. About half the returning women applicants need some form of remediation before they can begin nontraditional skills training. Based on past experience, the in-house approach to basic skill development has been the most effective. This method of teaching allows CBOs the flexibility to offer courses that run the gamut from basic literacy to simple math review. For example, Wider Opportunities for Women, in Washington, D.C., offers nontraditional skills training to women in several trades. No applicant is turned away. After an initial assessment, each applicant can be placed at an appropriate level in the program, whether it is in the actual skills training for which she originally applied or in a math review that will prepare her for the skills program. Because all applicants are accepted, they immediately form a bond and become committed to completing the training cycle, in spite of being placed in remediation at first. Wider Opportunities for Women can therefore enroll and retain a high percentage of its applicants.

Women who enter training programs sponsored by CBOs have a history of academic failure. This has left them wary of any further exposure to formal academic training, particularly when information is presented in lectures. Therefore, the most effective way to communicate the more abstract skills that trainees require (aspects of mathematics, blueprint reading and interpretation, English as a second language) is by application to their shop assignments. Teaching reentry women to cope with the hands-on aspects of their training also provides an excellent framework for teaching them to think analytically and solve problems. The theory they are taught is mastered through its application to real problems encountered in the training program's shops. Learning in this manner speeds the process of skill acquisition and serves to increase retention.

In Connecticut, where the majority of poor women have low functional literacy, training curricula generally integrate basic remediation (English, reading, writing, mathematics) with technical theory and hands-on skills development. Literacy classes that are oriented to career-related skills seem to be the best motivators for students who lack confidence in the classroom and who may lose interest in traditional remediation settings. Typically, the more relevant classes are to the job, the more successful trainees feel. Reading and writing classes offered in a vocationally oriented context incorporate trade vocabulary and descriptions of the day-to-day responsibilities of the job into all reading materials. Math is made less intimidating by an emphasis on the actual calculations that will be required on the job. Even the teaching of English as a second language is enhanced in a vocational context.

The most successful job-related training takes place in programs that are closely linked with the workplace. Every attempt is made to provide realistic on-the-job experiences in the curriculum. Frequent site visits to companies, guest speakers from industry, and contact with successful women graduates who are working in the field help women to develop a realistic understanding of the skills they are learning and the settings in which they will be working. Many nontraditional training programs offer an internship or "shadowing" component, during which each woman spends a period of time observing and sometimes assisting a worker in the field. This is particularly useful for women who are unfamiliar with the dynamics of the industrial workplace.

Some CBOs are able to develop training programs in conjunction with private industry. This approach has dual benefits. First, the probability of getting a job on completion of the program seems more real to the students. Second, industry feels an obligation to hire the women who complete the program. For example, the Hartford Area Training Center (HATC) developed a training program for a manufacturer of printed circuit boards. The company had been experiencing a high turnover rate in its inspection department. HATC, in conjunction with the company, developed a curriculum to train inspectors. The company lent HATC the necessary equipment. This training program was repeated three times, and the women who completed it were all placed in jobs with the company.

When a training program operates industrywide and is not tailored to the needs of one particular employer, the active involvement of private industry is necessary. This can be accomplished by having representatives from industry participate on advisory boards. These industrial representatives can provide training materials and up-to-date information about current technology. Some CBOs run their programs at technical colleges or vocational high schools because of the schools' existing ties with industry. For example, Hartford College for Women's program in cable TV installation training was run at Hartford State Technical College, using several of its faculty members and its electricity laboratories. An instructor from the Connecticut Light and Power Company taught pole-climbing techniques, the local cable company supplied vans for driving practice, and the electrical union offered a site for pole-climbing practice. Several cable companies across the state gave tours of their facilities and provided company personnel for training in interviewing skills. In addition, they allowed the women to work with their installers for a day to learn the daily responsibilities of installers. Such a cooperative venture is indicative of the potential for providing returning women with expanded training opportunities in nontraditional occupations.

Creating a Supportive Atmosphere

It is essential to create a supportive atmosphere where trainees feel respected for their work. Staff members must be sensitive to the needs of low-income, minority students. They must be clearly antiracist, antisexist, and respectful of the trainees and their cultural values and norms.

Training programs are most often composed of returning women from diverse sections of the population. The breadth of their backgrounds can have a dual effect on the classroom atmosphere. On the one hand, the trainees with successful work or educational histories, as well as those who grasp technical theory most easily, can serve as role models and motivators for other, less proficient classmates. On the other hand, the more successful trainees can also be intimidating to their peers. It is not unusual for successful individuals to adopt a patronizing approach in helping their classmates by doing difficult tasks for them. Despite good intentions, this actually impedes the learning process. It is essential that a spirit of cooperation and "can do" permeate the classroom and the shop. In this spirit, the more advanced trainees should be encouraged to assist in teaching their classmates, but not to do tasks for them. Rather, they should show how and why. This also helps women overcome the patronizing attitudes they tend to encounter in nontraditional work environments.

Program Design

In general, training programs should be run like the workplaces for which students are preparing, but with more encouragement and flexibility. Reentry women, in particular, respond well to high expectations from the staff. Rules and regulations must be explained and enforced, and high standards must be maintained. Many CBOs have found that the most effective structure for skills training is a flexible, open-entry, open-exit model. It allows participants to enter the program at frequent intervals, to leave when they have accomplished the program training goals, and to learn at their own pace in an individualized mode. Because of scheduling needs and the changing circumstances of women's lives, particularly among women with primary childcare responsibilities, an open-entry, open-exit structure is ideal. For returning women, who often encounter problems that cause them to drop out, an open-entry, open-exit structure allows them to return when their difficulties are resolved.

To design open-entry, open-exit programming, the staff must develop clear, competency-based training objectives for each component of the program and communicate them to the trainees. This not only holds CBO instructors accountable but also provides clear and measurable educational goals for trainees. The same goals can be used to structure the ongoing feedback that trainees receive from the staff.

The choice of staffing for a CBO's nontraditional training program is critical to its success. Each staff member must be sensitive to the special needs of returning women, as well as to low-income and minority populations. While some staff members may need to be bilingual, the entire staff must be able to convey a sense of respect for the trainees and their cultures. Whenever possible, it is best to hire role models: female and minority instructors and administrators who can develop immediate rapport with trainees and convey understanding of their situations. Tutors must also be available to trainees who fall behind in their studies. Once again, a supportive atmosphere, along with individual attention, increases persistence.

Counseling

The counseling component of any training program is critical to the success of returning women, particularly those who have had limited success in prior educational settings. Therefore, it is extremely important for nontraditional training programs to have full-time, on-site counselors available to trainees. Class scheduling should allow for academic, personal, and career counseling to take place, on both a structured and an impromptu basis, throughout the training. Initial orientation sessions should familiarize trainees with the role of counselors and encourage trainees to seek assistance with their problems and concerns.

It is important that a counselor regularly schedule appointments with each woman to discuss her progress in the program. These sessions provide an opportunity to explore any special support needs that arise and to discuss how the student is coping with the increased demands placed on her family by the training. While trainees are encouraged to seek out the counselor during class hours if a pressing need arises, it is the counselor's role to actively pursue trainees who are experiencing difficulty in the classroom or whose absences indicate special support needs.

Academic counseling must be done on a regular basis to help returning women set realistic goals that match their career objectives. Those with poor academic histories, math anxiety, or a fear of testing may need special encouragement and attention. Self-advocacy is also encouraged, so that students can learn to handle their own problems. In particular, students are encouraged to work out on their own any problems that may arise with their instructors.

A great deal of personal counseling is required during a nontraditional training program. The lack of confidence often displayed by women who have been out of school for a long time is acute and may initially be debilitating. An on-site counselor can intervene to help women work through their fear of failure, to provide encouragement to those who believe they are too old to learn, and to listen to those who do not believe they can handle added pressures at home or who feel guilty about investing family time and resources in their own training. If a few trainees require more intensive therapy, the counselor can link them with appropriate services. When there are men in the class, an ongoing support group just for women provides a comfortable space for female trainees to share concerns, strategize solutions, and offer encouragement to one another. In the group, the women discover that they share similar concerns. Some experience resistance from their children and partners to their enrollment in the program; others feel intimidated by the hands-on technical component. Such issues are raised and openly discussed, and students feel less isolated with their problems and can take advantage of solutions other women have found effective.

Placement

The goal of reentry women who enter skills training is employment upon completion. The promise of employment is the motivation that helps them to weather the hardships they face in order to remain in the training. Nevertheless, the returning women who enter training programs have many barriers to employment, including spotty work records, histories of tardiness and absenteeism, police records, inadequate and unstable childcare, lack of transportation, poor interviewing skills, lack of confidence, and unreal expectations. Some have no previous work experience or career goals. In addition, women training for nontraditional fields face the sexist and racist attitudes of employers. CBOs must have several means of helping women overcome these barriers. Two of the most effective are placement specialists and World of Work classes.

Placement Specialists

Upon completion of training, two approaches to placement are utilized by CBOs: placement assistance and placement. Placement assistance requires applicants to make their own contacts with employers and set up their own interviews. Individuals are often given leads by the CBO staff, but they are generally on their own. In contrast, placement, as practiced by many CBOs, uses a skilled staff member to make contacts with employers. Placement specialists visit job sites to learn what particular employers are seeking. They become experts on job availability and career ladders within specific trades. Because of their knowledge, placement specialists can often match particular women to particular jobs.

Experience has shown several advantages to having an in-house placement person. The placement specialist knows the women, their strengths, and their weaknesses. On the basis of knowledge about and interactions with the women, the placement person can identify the most appropriate job and job setting for each one. There is a greater likelihood of trainees' success when there are good matches. The placement specialist develops close ties with industry. This ensure continual feedback on how graduates are performing. It also allows the CBO to intervene with a graduate and provide support, as necessary. Moreover, the consistent realiability of recommendations made by the placement specialist leads to respect for the program and its trainees, as well as to more jobs.

The role of the placement specialist has become increasingly clear in the Hartford job-skills training network. In the early 1980s, placement in the Hartford area was done by a centralized office. The Private Industry Council-sponsored training programs referred trainees to a single office, where all categories of jobs were being developed. The Hartford Area Training Center (one of the Private Industry Council's sponsored training programs), a precision-machine training program, found itself in a tight labor market. Many experienced workers were being laid off from the aircraft industry. It was difficult to place trainees and, since placement is a key measure of success in training programs that have funders, the program was in trouble. The Private Industry Council could not and did not provide the special attention and advocacy needed to place trainees under these conditions, nor did it have the time or focus to develop a relationship with individual employers in each field. Therefore, the Hartford Area Training Center itself began to develop jobs for its own trainees. Since that time, a placement specialist has been on staff and is considered vital to the program's ongoing success.

World of Work

The job-seeking skills classes, sometimes called World of Work (WOW) classes, are a critical counseling tool to prepare trainees for job placement. The World of Work class addresses the many problems reentry women face in getting and keeping jobs. In this class, trainees discuss ways to overcome barriers to their success, and each trainee develops tactics that will help her overcome her own particular obstacles. Confidence comes first from having mastered vocational skills, and second from the atmosphere of encouragement and confidence that permeates the program.

It is essential that World of Work classes address both personal and employment-related issues. Women who are entering new jobs, particularly those in nontraditional fields, need practice in on-the-job survival techniques. World of Work classes train women to recognize and handle workplace politics: to avoid and resolve conflicts, to be assertive, to work through unions, and to know their rights as workers. Because CBOs frequently deal with the dynamics of the racist, sexist, and antigay attitudes graduates face on the job, role playing and case studies are used to help women develop effective responses to sexual and racial harassment, as well as to the surprisingly widespread phenomenon of gay-baiting.

For example, students in Hartford College for Women's program in cable TV installation were intentionally mixed by gender, age, and ethnicity. Rather than focusing separately on sexual or racial harassment, the World of Work classes addressed the dynamics of discrimination on the job. The instructors found that individual trainees were not put on the defensive by this approach, and that they were able to see the dynamics of discrimination and how it had worked to disempower all of them for different reasons. They were able to relate to specific incidents in which they had been the targets of discrimination. They could then go on to develop responses to each type of discrimination.

Besides attending to discrimination in the workplace, instructors must also be sensitized to signs of harassment in class. White and heterosexual trainees often make "harmless" comments of jokes about the black, Hispanic, and lesbian trainees. Such behavior must be pointed out. It must be made clear that this kind of undermining treatment is not acceptable in the classroom. Although there is often initial resistance, trainees can and do learn to treat one another with respect, if respect is continually modeled and enforced.

In the World of Work class, trainees are encouraged to develop specific vocational goals, including both long-term career goals and the interim steps to reach them. Employers and past graduates are often invited to address the class and to communicate the importance of having employees who are reliable, who follow instructions, who continue to learn on the job, and who demonstrate positive work attitudes. Classes also raise the issues of workplace safety, the role of the Occupational Safety and Health Administration, and apprenticeship opportunities.

Follow-up

The unique relationship between the CBO and returning women students is exempified by the program's relationship with the trainees after graduation and during job placement. The CBO continues to monitor a woman's progress and adjustment to her new job and changed life. Typical ongoing "retention services" for graduates include prescribed contacts with graduates and employers at one week, three weeks, three months, and six months. If there are problems on the job, CBO staff will meet with the graduates and the employer to achieve resolution. When sexual harassment has been reported, the CBO staff will meet with the graduate to determine what action, if any, she wishes to pursue. The staff will help her follow through on whatever decision she makes.

All graduates are encouraged to keep in touch with the program staff and offer feedback on how to make training more relevant to jobs. Because employers tend to call job developers about job openings, placement is an ongoing service, both for those currently in the program and for those who have graduated. Graduates who are looking for better jobs contact trainers to keep abreast of job openings. Notification of apprenticeship openings, as well as information regarding membership in professional organizations, are also mailed to all graduates.

Potluck dinners are vehicles for maintaining contact and are held two months and six months after graduation. Potlucks give the women an informal setting to discuss problems and allow them to share their on-the-job experiences. In addition to such informal gatherings, many CBOs, particularly those that train for nontraditional occupations, run ongoing support groups for their graduates. The support groups continue to provide graduates with information about new jobs and classes, for upgrading skills. Guest speakers from industry, programs on how to balance work with parenting responsibilities, and speakers from professional organizations all provide a forum for skill development. Graduates feel close ties to these programs, and the fact that women return year after year underscores the efficacy of the structures that are in place.

The effectiveness of CBO training programs for returning women can be measured in several ways. One is that within six to eight months, women whose lives have been without any real productive outlook become highly skilled workers with broad career opportunities. Second, trainees who complete the programs remain loyal and return for frequent visits. Finally, women who were once characterized as dependent and having low self-esteem emerge as self-directed, efficacious, self-confident, and productive employees.

Ruth S. Howell is education coordinator of the State Department of Income Maintenance in Hartford, Connecticut, and former director of nontraditional training at Hartford College for Women.

Helen Schwartz is assistant director of the Hartford Area Training Center and former placement specialist for the center.

Displaced homemakers and rural, minority, and disabled women bring to their education and pretraining programs particular needs that require specific accommodations.

Women from Special Populations: The Challenge of Reentry

Phyllis C. Safman

Reentry implies a return to work or school after a lapse of time. The term connotes excitement and anxiety, for it refers to change that promises self-improvement, fulfilled dreams, and a better life. The promise of a better life, in whatever form it takes, appeals to thousands of women who return to the workforce or to school, or who participate in training programs. For others, the promise is obscure. There are women who enter pretraining programs and bring with them myriad problems that must be addressed before the promise becomes a personal dream. These women are displaced homemakers, rural dwellers, and ethnic and racial

---

The information contained in this chapter came from the experience and wisdom of women who are or were intimately involved with these programs. I offer sincere thanks to Virginia Kelson, executive director, Phoenix Institute (Salt Lake City); Dr. Joan Goldberg, project facilitator, Rural Women's Work Readiness Project (Syracuse); Judith Patrick, associate director, Mi Casa Resource Center for Women (Denver); and Olga Nadeau, coordinator, Center for Disabled Student Services at the University of Utah (Salt Lake City). Others who were willing to contribute their experiences and to whom I am grateful are Mary Nielson, Debra Mair, Jane Carbine, and Jaydine Merkel.

minorities. They are joined by physically disabled women, who bring to educational settings yet another set of problems that must be addressed.

What makes these groups unique? Displaced homemakers are women who have operated in a family sphere, only to find themselves with children and without their partners' financial support, because of divorce, desertion, disability, or death, and without marketable skills. Rural women, who are often displaced homemakers and single mothers, have few options and resources available to them in their small communities. Minority women may be living within ethnic communities with strong cultural traditions, but without responsible partners and adequate resources. Disabled women experience a unique set of limitations and face barriers unrecognized by their physically able counterparts.

The experiences of these women are explained through four programs: the Displaced Homemakers Project of Phoenix Institute, Salt Lake City, Utah; the Rural Women's Work Readiness Project, Onondaga Community College, Syracuse, New York; Mi Casa Resource Center for Women, Denver, Colorado; and the Center for Disabled Student Services, University of Utah, Salt Lake City. This chapter includes a description of each of these programs, the special needs of the women participants, and each program's efforts to accommodate those needs. The case-study approach is not meant to be a definitive description of reentry women with special needs. Instead, it is intended to provide insight into the particular needs of specific women so that professionals in continuing education and training programs can better understand and accommodate the needs of their current and future clients. In the instance of minorities, only Chicana women from one program are represented, yet racial and ethnic minorities participate in all the other programs. A close look at the four programs and their participants not only illuminates the challenges of reentry faced by these special populations but also provides insights on how the reentry transition can be facilitated.

The Displaced Homemakers Project

Program Description

The Displaced Homemakers Project is housed in the Phoenix Institute, a nonprofit career and employment training center that opened its doors in 1971. Working with politicians and business executives, the executive director of Phoenix Institute helped to obtain passage of the 1986 Utah Displaced Homemakers Act, funded by a twenty-dollar assessed fee on marriage licenses, which provides job-related services to displaced homemakers. Over 50 percent of the states have such acts on their books, although the sources and amounts of appropriations vary.

The purpose of the Displaced Homemakers Project is to facilitate economic independence through a program of pretraining. The program includes extensive individual and group counseling, assertiveness training, anger management, career planning, résumé writing, communication skills, interviewing techniques, interest and ability testing, assistance with problem solving, and referrals to community resources. Individual and group therapies are funded by United Way, while the other classes are funded by appropriations from the Utah Displaced Homemakers Act. During an initial interview, a woman's needs are assessed and a self-sufficiency plan is developed, inclusive of the varied program offerings. Approximately three hundred women have been served since the project was funded in February 1987.

The project is staffed by one part-time therapist and two interns. Recruitment practices include referrals from community agencies and from women who are participating or have participated in the program. In addition, the executive director uses television and press coverage to reach women in need and others who know of women in need. She says that television is an effective medium because displaced homemakers are isolated at home with their televisions and have extremely limited activities, all close to home.

Participants' Characteristics

The women who enter the Phoenix Institute's Displaced Homemakers Project average forty years of age, with children between the ages of five and twelve. They tend to live in their own homes with their children, and most are not receiving public assistance. Those who do receive public assistance are eligible for Job Training Partnership Act (JTPA) stipends. The homogeneity of Utah's population (70 percent Mormon) is reflected in the project's ethnic profile: 88 percent are Caucasian. Hispanic women account for only 5 percent, while Native Americans and black women make up 4 percent of the population. Legislative guidelines require a woman to have been out of the workforce for ten years in order to qualify for the project. The executive director is working with the legislature to reduce the number of years required for eligibility.

One-quarter of the women are high school dropouts. Many perform poorly in math, and most have limited knowledge of computers. All the women who enter the program do so for economic reasons: they find themselves without adequate income or skills to obtain economic stability.

Psychosocial Characteristics

One woman said, "I was devastated when I went to Phoenix. Life was supposed to take off after the divorce because the problem was gone. I couldn't pull myself out of devastation." *Confused, depressed,* and *angry* are three adjectives used by the staff to describe displaced homemakers. Their confusion comes in part from living in a culture that places a great emphasis on women's roles as wives and mothers. Another woman has said, "I lost hope for making the family work. That was all I ever wanted." When the partner leaves or dies, the homemaker is thrust out of a comfortable and socially acceptable role. She is unprepared to alter that role. Having seen herself as a mother and helpmate, she has paid no attention to career options or development: "When I was growing up, all the girls wanted to be wives and mothers."

Seeing themselves as failures, and confused by the loss of the homemaker role, the women isolate themselves and often show signs of depression. Self-esteem is shattered, and feelings of helplessness replace the security of a husband's presence and financial support. Those who enter the project come without career goals. They enter with only their confusion, depression, anger, and a sense that they have nothing and are nothing: "I felt like I was in a hole and couldn't get out. I was unworthy, desperate, and angry. I grew up thinking you stayed married."

Poor self-esteem leads to another struggle: They want to remain dependent but know they must become independent. The partner that encouraged dependency is gone. Thus, poor self-esteem, confusion, depression, and conflict over dependency characterize the displaced homemakers who enter Phoenix Institute.

Program Accommodations

Self-Esteem. A woman with the characteristics just described is likely to spend eight weeks in individual and group therapy. The purpose of the individual therapy is to help her accept her situation, discover her own strengths, and rebuild her shattered self-esteem. Group therapy provides an opportunity for women in similar situations to learn from each other how to handle difficult family relationships, express feelings, and develop support networks where each person is accepted and valued.

Assertiveness training teaches skills that help women move from being passive recipients to being active managers of their lives. A month-long course on anger management helps women to understand the source of their anger and develop skills to redirect their energies.

Childcare. The Utah Displaced Homemakers Act provides only short-term or crisis-care reimbursement for childcare costs. Typically, the women require after-school care for their children. Staff members try to help the women identify suitable childcare options.

Literacy. Women who lack basic literacy skills are identified by the staff, who in turn refer them to local adult basic education programs. These programs exist in every district throughout the city and are easily accessible.

Job Preparation. Once literacy skills are sharpened, the women study résumé writing and job-interview skills. Phoenix Institute receives numerous calls from prospective employers who see displaced homemakers as potentially valuable employees: The perception is that these women are unlikely to get pregnant or to have very young children or to move to accommodate a husband's career. The attitudes of some perspective employers are based on stereotypic assumptions regarding women's lives. Such sexist attitudes often predispose employers to hire older women. Thus, a conundrum exists whereby the displaced homemaker's maturity and life experience may enhance her employability but also limit opportunities for younger women.

Training of Staff. Staff training is based on the needs of the women served by the project. Low self-esteem and the tendency toward dependence, first on their partners and then on staff, prompted the development of a three-tier assertive communication program. Each staff member participates in sessions on assertiveness versus aggressiveness, nonverbal communication, resolving conflict, anger management, and other topics designed to turn participants' dependence into independence through skills training and appropriate modeling behavior.

Barriers to Success

Commitment to the Program. Refusal to make a full commitment to the program, and the inability to resolve dependency needs, are cited by staff as the major barriers that affect a woman's successful transition from homemaker to wage earner. Turning around almost forty years of acculturation poses a challenge for participants and staff.

Funding. Funding to maintain and expand existing programs is currently inadequate. Resources are unavailable to conduct follow-up interviews and develop support groups, both on site and in local neighborhoods, for women who complete the program. Support groups are seen as a very powerful tool for helping women to continue their progress. Directly related to funding is the issue of time. The participants require more time than funding allows to make an adequate transition from being homemakers to being wage earners.

Without adequate funding, women will stay in their same situations, unable to get the adequate pretraining necessary to make them independent and contributing members of their communities.

Rural Women's Work Readiness Project

The Rural Women's Work Readiness Project, a demonstration project funded by the New York State Department of Education, was implemented in 1985 in three rural communities in Onondaga County, in central New York. Its purpose was to provide comprehensive educational services to rural women in need. All participants met JTPA financial eligibility requirements. Many were displaced homemakers. The demonstration project was directed by the Center for Community Education at Onondaga Community College in Syracuse.

Program Description

This pretraining demonstration project was designed to enable participants to gain access to needed services and become aware of education, training, and employment options. A unique linkage system brought to the three rural sites representatives from such agencies as the Onondaga Child Care Council, the Cooperative Extension Service, the New York State Division of Human Rights, the YWCA, and the Onondaga County Employment and Training Agency. Through the linkages, participants learned about the services, as well as about consumer economics, physical fitness and nutrition, health, budgeting, employment opportunities, childcare options, parenting skills, and related home and workplace issues. In return, the agency representatives developed a better understanding of the needs and issues of low-income rural women.

In addition, the program offered skills assessment, career exploration, goal setting, job-market assessment, time management, stress management, résumé preparation, job-seeking skills, and interviewing and educational counseling (which included testing, evaluation, and referral). The five-week program involved participants from each rural site for six hours daily, Monday through Friday.

The grant and matching funds covered the cost of one full-time program facilitator and several part-time staff members who were responsible for advocacy, coordination, financial management, and counseling on educational resources. Transportation and childcare costs were reimbursed to the participants.

Although 125 eligible women were identified and contacted, 36 entered the program and 22 actually completed all five weeks. Recruitment was a multifaceted effort. Lists of women on public assistance, and of those with children in Head Start programs, were obtained. In one rural town, an outreach worker from the local parish called a meeting of eligible women to inform them of the program. Women who had completed the program spoke with women in the other rural areas before the next five-week session.

Participants' Characteristics

Of the thirty-six women who participated in the project, 94 percent were between twenty-two and forty-four years old, and 47 percent had dependent children. Half of the women held high school diplomas. With the exception of 19 percent who were Native American, all were Caucasian. Most of the women were single heads of households, although some lived with male partners.

Psychosocial Characteristics

The women reported feelings of degradation because of their dependence on public assistance and the problems inherent in working with that system. They also cited boredom as a reason for participation in the project. Like their counterparts in the Displaced Homemakers Project, they did not come with career goals; they knew only that they wanted something other than what they currently had.

The women tended to be isolated from services and from other women like themselves. Their feelings of degradation, boredom, and isolation contributed to their low self-esteem. In addition, many of these women had been or were currently abused by their partners. A typical abused woman internalizes the abuser's view of her; she sees herself as inadequate, incapable, and deserving of abuse (Walker, 1983). Abused women also tend to become dependent, not trusting themselves to make decisions or move forward with their lives.

Program Accommodations

Linkages. The women were introduced to education and training options through the field trips they took to the community college and training programs in Syracuse. While visiting the college, the women spoke with female students, financial aid officers, and academic advisers. Visiting the training programs, they held conversations with instructors and trainees. The field trips not only demonstrated available options for education and employment but also removed any preconceived barriers. Women like themselves were in school and on the job; these options were accessible.

Self-Esteem. Back in their rural classrooms, the women involved themselves with sessions on confidence building and assertiveness training. They also met with representatives from various agencies. During one of those meetings, the project participants, one by one, began leaving the room for a cigarette. After the speaker left, the facilitator queried the participants on their unusual behavior. Several of the women admitted to embarrassment and discomfort at hearing scenarios they knew only too well. The speaker was from a shelter for battered women. Thereafter, group sessions became a forum for the discussion of abuse and its effects on self-esteem.

Job Preparation. Pretraining activities engaged the women in résumé writing and interview skills. Educational testing revealed strengths and needs. Job requirements for various fields were investigated. Each woman developed a plan of action that was assessed two months after the five-week session. Nine women planned to go to college and saw their plans realized.

Sensitization. During the program, the women became sensitized to the political issues that affected their lives. Some lobbied the New York state legislature on childcare issues. Others advised women in their communities about services and career options. Still others learned to address community groups on the plight of low-income, rural women.

Barriers to Success

Attrition. Thirty-six women began the three programs, and twenty-two completed the five-week commitment. One group of twelve dwindled to four. A combination of cultural pull, lack of commitment to the program, and family and other pressures probably contributed to the attrition among those who left.

Self-Esteem. Continual dependence of some of the women on abusive men slowed down the process of building self-esteem. The women learned to be assertive with each other and, as the program facilitator indicated, "they talked a good game." Their behavior at home, however, appeared to lag behind the insights they demonstrated with their peers. Still, the content and dynamics of the project created new self-awareness. If the project did not foster change, it did impart the knowledge that change is possible.

Funding. Delays of several months shortened the recruitment process. Initially, reimbursements for childcare and transportation were late, which hampered the women's ability to pay for these services. Once the project was terminated, of course, women who did not obtain employment were left isolated in their rural communities and without funding for childcare and transportation.

Although Onondaga Community College Center for Community Education received an award from the National Association of Counties for this project, additional funding has not been forthcoming. Nevertheless, two separate groups are currently seeking funding to replicate this project in two rural sites in the state.

Mi Casa Resource Center for Women

Program Description

Mi Casa Resource Center for Women is in a Chicano neighborhood on the west side of Denver. Its mission is to serve women with low incomes. Mi Casa acts as a bridge between the women's homes and the world of work. This eleven-year-old agency serves approximately six hundred women per year, with a staff of ten full-time and two half-time employees. The ethnic makeup of the staff and trainers reflects sensitivity to the needs of the Chicana women: nine Chicanas, two anglos, and one black woman provide advocacy and training. Crisis advocacy for housing, food, clothes, and health care is included along with individual and group counseling. Job-readiness skills, résumé preparation, and interviewing are offered along with assertiveness training. Staff members perform educational testing to assess skill levels. A GED program is offered on site for community members who wish to obtain high school diplomas.

This one-week intensive program is funded through JTPA, United Way, and other granting agencies. Recruitment of Chicana women is done through leaflets and an outreach thrust that takes staff into housing projects and safe houses (shelters for battered women). Trainers conduct inservice sessions in other agencies to acquaint their staffs with the needs of Chicana women and the services provided by Mi Casa. Program participants are very effective recruiters of their peers and family members.

Participants' Characteristics

The women who come to Mi Casa tend to be between twenty-one and thirty-nine years old and to be single parents. Approximately 66 percent have yearly incomes under five thousand dollars. The majority, 76 percent, are Chicana, and 15 percent are Caucasian. The other 9 percent include black, Native American, and Asian women.

Since only 36 percent have completed high school, some of the women lack adequate literacy skills; others speak only Spanish. To accommodate both groups, staff and trainers are bilingual, and a woman may elect to have materials read to her.

Reasons for entering the week-long job-readiness program vary with the needs and sophistication of the women. Some simply articulate a need to get into a training program, while others enter Mi Casa expecting to be handed a job. At the other extreme are those who want staff to guess their needs, which often include housing, food, medical care, and clothing.

Psychosocial Characteristics

Many women enter the program confused, angry, and low in self-esteem. They worry about survival. They lack marketable skills and understanding of the business world. Many are or were abused by their partners.

The Chicana women share several characteristics. First, their partners and families exert pressure on them to remain in the home and away from the workforce. Second, community members share traditional values, which place women in a passive and subservient role, while men are dominant. Consequently, Chicana women in the program appear to be less assertive than other women. Third, most of the women have never interacted in groups composed entirely of women who are not family members. Thus, strong traditional values and family ties often contribute to passivity among Chicana women.

Program Accommodations

Pretraining Assessment. Every woman who enters Mi Casa receives an interview, to assess her personal and pretraining needs, and a two-hour orientation to the program. Those eligible for JTPA stipends are identified, and those who need public assistance are guided through the social service systems. Educational testing, conducted by staff members, indicates the women's strengths and needs. Women with literacy problems are encouraged to enroll in local adult basic education programs.

Job Preparation. Participants involve themselves in testing, career counseling, job searches, and sessions designed to address their lack of knowledge about employment, finances, and self-management. Before the last day of the one-week training program, each woman practices an interview session with a trainer before a video camera. This allows the prospective employee to review her performance and, with the help of the trainer, improve her interview skills. Job-search support groups are held weekly for those who complete the program but are still unemployed. A counseling group, with the euphemism "assertiveness class," also meets weekly. (The term *counseling* is not readily accepted in the Chicano homes of these particular women.) A course on auto mechanics is offered once a year. The staff is proud of its success rate: Of the women who complete the one-week pretraining program, 75 percent obtain employment.

Self-Esteem. Staff members and trainers address participants' self-esteem through assertiveness training and counseling. Nine Chicana staff members and trainers provide role models for participants unfamiliar with successful and career-oriented Chicana women.

Barriers to Success

Poor Self-Esteem. Some women leave the program right before the videotaping session. Trying a new skill (interviewing) and risking failure both require a strong self-concept. One week of intense training is not long enough to strengthen fragile self-esteem that has been eroded by a partner or that has had little opportunity for development in a rigid and traditional atmosphere.

Childcare. High-quality affordable childcare is a continuous problem for low-income women. Caretakers who are willing to address the personal and educational needs of the children are difficult to find.

Cultural Pull. These particular Chicana women have grown up with traditional role expectations. Mothers model these roles, and fathers reinforce them. Add to the mix an abusive partner. Often strong role expectations and lack of resources keep women in their current situations even when violence is present.

Immigration Laws. Chicana women may also be victimized by the new immigration laws. Mi Casa has found that some prospective employers assume that all brown-skinned people are illegal aliens. Therefore, employers are reluctant to hire Chicana women. Fortunately, not all employers express this bias; 75 percent of the women do find employment.

Center for Disabled Student Services

Program Description

"I wanted to be a beautician and raise a family," a woman relates. "The accident changed all that. I had no choice but to go to college." The Center for Disabled Student Services at the University of Utah opened in 1973. Its purpose is to help students with disabilities make optimal use of their university experience. The center provides whatever resources are necessary for students to participate in academic and nonacademic activities equally with able-bodied students. It serves students who have mobility, visual, and hearing impairments and those with learning disabilities. Physical disability may have occurred at birth, or later, from an accident or a disease. All students who make use of the center have diagnostic verification of their disabilities on file.

The center staff provides assistance with registration, scheduling, counseling, advocacy, referrals, orientation, housing, childcare, transportation, and equipment. Students are given help in obtaining wheelchairs, tape recorders, and other aids. Its funding comes through a line-item appropriation. Staff includes a full-time coordinator, a part-time secretary, and two half-time counselors for students with learning disabilities. There is a state-funded rehabilitation-services coordinator, who has a part-time secretary.

An estimated 150 students use the center every quarter, although the number of participants drops in winter. Approximately 50 percent of the students are female, the majority of whom are reentering after having suffered disabilities. The rest of the female students enter directly from high school. The university actively recruits students who have disabilities.

Participants' Characteristics

The women who use the center range in age from eighteen to sixty-five. The homogeneity of Utah's population, as mentioned earlier, is reflected in the center's ethnic breakdown. All the current students are white, with the exception of three Asian women, two black women, and one Chicana woman. Typically, the women who were disabled at birth or very early in life are not married. If the disability occurred later, they are likely to be divorced with children. Although wheelchair-accessible housing is not always easy to find, most of these reentry women live independently. Some hire attendants to help with bodily needs. Disabilities may be caused by visual and hearing impairments, diabetes, spinal cord impairment due to injury or disease, multiple sclerosis, cerebral palsy, heart and lung problems, brain trauma, or severe allergies.

Students with physical disabilities who are eligible carry Social Security Disability Insurance. The Division of Rehabilitation Services may assist with tuition, books, and medical needs. Some students obtain Pell Grants that can be applied toward their tuition. Unique to this center are two scholarships that are offered to students with disabilities: the Louise Snow Scholarship and the American Handicapped Workers Foundation Scholarship.

These women and men return to school for financial reasons. While a student remains in school, medical and financial support for tuition, books, and housing are available along with the center's resources. Students also seek advanced degrees, which will provide a competitive edge in the job market. Thus, available resources and the promise of advanced credentials are powerful magnets that attract and keep these students in school.

Psychosocial Characteristics

A young woman who is born with a disability depends on her family to interpret the world and its reaction to her. Often, disabled female children are sheltered, protected, and discouraged from taking the risks that lead to independence. They are made to feel vulnerable and incapable of venturing out into the world. It is no wonder that these same young women begin adulthood without strong self-esteem. When a woman has become disabled later in life because of injury or disease, her family and significant others play a major role in her acceptance of herself. Often, her husband leaves, and the woman must fend for herself and her children. In these cases, self-esteem is more dependent on her ability to handle her children and everyday life. Thus, the woman's capability, and the messages she receives from those in her world, will affect her view of herself and her self-esteem.

The center finds that the students do not bond easily with one another. Some women protect their space and discourage any effort by others to touch them, their wheelchairs, their guide dogs, or their canes. Others segregate themselves from able-bodied students. During social mixers held at the center, staff members note that students tend to congregate with others of like disability: The deaf separate themselves from those in wheelchairs, who separate themselves from the blind. People with speech problems are often discounted.

Program Accommodation

Scheduling. Much time is spent in teaching students how to plan their schedules, given their special limitations and personal needs. Planning is critical to the accommodation of curriculum requirements, class location, and such architectural barriers as stairs. Women with children are advised on how to balance class schedules, travel, and childcare demands. The center handles registration in its office, arranges for textbook delivery, and provides tutors, readers, scribes, and technological aids. It also works with the financial aid office to arrange for grants and disability allotments.

Advocacy. The center must often serve as a liaison with other units on campus and intercede on behalf of disabled students. Working with the university's scheduling office, the center often has rooms changed to accommodate the physical limitations of students. Staff members talk with departments and instructors to arrange for tests to be given at the center, where the need for additional time and special aids, such as readers, can be accommodated.

Socialization. The center sponsors mixers to encourage socializing by the students. Unfortunately, women with dependent children are likely to be less able to take advantage of these occasions.

Every year the Center sponsors a dinner that recognizes the achievements of the students. A professionally successful guest who has a disability is invited to address the group and interact with the students. Finding role models for the students, particularly the women, is a task the staff considers very important.

Barriers to Success

Self-Esteem. Women who were not encouraged early to become independent, and who have difficulty adjusting to a physical disability, tend to have poor self-esteem. Poor self-esteem hampers their ability to bond with others and may impede their efforts to succeed in school and obtain employment.

Acknowledgment of Disability. Some women and men refuse to acknowledge their disabilities and are uncomfortable if others do. For instance, a woman may become defensive if an able-bodied person opens a door for her. Others will not use the center or its services. Women and men who acknowledge their disabilities and accept their limitations tend to make more satisfactory adjustments in their personal and professional lives.

Realistic Goal Setting. Because of financial limitations and the need for more time, students with physical disabilities do not have the luxury of sampling academic majors before choosing one. In addition, some fields require abilities that do not fit well with some physical disabilities. The student must make a realistic appraisal of her strengths and talents and choose a field that values these same attributes. Some nontraditional fields associated with science, math, architecture, and computer science may offer more opportunities for disabled women who are willing to forgo traditional paths.

Discrimination. Attitudes that lead to subtle and not-so-subtle discrimination abound. The able-bodied population tends to connect disability with inability or incompetence. While such companies as IBM and American Express seek out qualified employees with disabilities, most companies do not. Consequently, the likelihood of the physically disabled woman or man finding employment is not very good. The center reports that only half the students who graduate find employment. The struggles and persistence of people with disabilities do not remove the discrimination that many endure.

Discussion

As indicated in the foregoing discussion, all four groups—displaced homemakers, rural and minority women, and women with disabilities—share many of the same characteristics. Many come to adult education and pretraining programs with poor self-esteem, conflict about dependence, financial problems, issues regarding childcare, and physical limitations. As they develop skills to cope with the changes in their lives and redirect their energies, reentry women begin to recognize their potential and realize new dreams.

Availability and Accessibility. The adult education system can help to move these women through transition and into a place of self-sufficiency, a place where the dream takes shape. Classes may be made available at times and locations that are convenient and accessible. Time and transportation considerations may necessitate an outreach plan that uses existing facilities (accessible to people with disabilities) in local communities, particularly in rural settings.

Support Services. Support services that reflect an understanding of the needs of special populations are critical. Trained counselors, both academic and personal, and sympathetic staff who will help women get through the financial aid and admission/registration processes will greatly facilitate their entry into educational programs. Preparatory classes in study skills, time management, and assertiveness may also address some of the present and ongoing needs of these women. In addition, staff and faculty who are accessible, and who create an atmosphere of caring and support for the women, contribute to their persistence in educational settings.

Marketing. Special populations seem unlikely to enter continuing education programs unless creative marketing attracts them. Displaced homemakers can be reached through regional pretraining centers. Rural women can be approached through county service providers and local churches. Women from ethnic minorities can be targeted through their neighborhood centers and ethnic organizations. Women who have physical disabilities can be identified through rehabilitation services and patient education programs. Educational programs that make the effort to reach reentry women from special populations and to provide needed support services are more likely to find these women enrolling and persisting in academic settings.

Supportive Learning Environments. The supportive environment set by the educational program must extend into the classroom. Sensitive faculty who build on women's strengths contribute to the development of positive self-esteem. Adequate resources, learning aids, and time for understanding and completion of assignments promote successful experiences. Every success, no matter how small, strengthens the student's self-concept.

Consortial Development. Outside the classroom, directors of continuing education programs, particularly those in community colleges, may want to identify potential employers from nontraditional fields in order to develop consortia for education and job training. The benefits may include development of training programs in nontraditional fields where pay is higher, encouragement of prospective employers to create work environments where the needs of single parents for childcare and flextime are accommodated, and the education of prospective employers on issues of discrimination against Chicana women and women with disabilities.

Conclusion

The development of education, training, and employment opportunities for women from special populations is a challenge. Their needs require special accommodations so that self-sufficiency becomes a reality. The real challenge, however, is the prevention of an underclass of economically deprived women. Narrow definitions of roles, imposed on some women by their cultures, religious organizations, and families, often preclude educational growth and attainment. Physical abuse and discrimination erode women's self confidence and ability to become independent.

For now, continuing educators must respond to the immediate needs of women from special populations. In this way, the educational process will contribute to women's ability to change their lives. In turn, women will model for their children and others self-defined roles that speak of struggle, independence, and hope for realizing their dreams.

Reference

Walker, L. "The Battered Woman Syndrome Study." In D. Finkelhor and others (eds.), *The Dark Side of Families*. Newbury Park, Calif.: Sage, 1983.

Phyllis C. Safman is assistant dean of the Division of Continuing Education, University of Utah, Salt Lake City.

One way of acquiring, maintaining, and demonstrating competence is to develop a network of supportive relationships to assist in the accomplishment of goals and successful transitions.

Extending an Invitation to Returning Women

Linda H. Lewis

It is clear from the information presented in this sourcebook that a woman's decision to continue her education implies changes and questions, accompanied by the emergence of major tasks that need to be accomplished. Concerns about her physical appearance, her ability to compete successfully, her role as a mother, spouse, or significant other, and her awareness of time limitations are but a few examples of the issues a reentry woman confronts and seeks to resolve. Reappraisal of the past and modification of life structure become part of the developmental progression as returning women engage in a continual process of individuation. Some are fortunate and receive considerable support during this transitional period; others, however, experience their developmental concerns in isolation and sometimes encounter negative feedback when they return to school.

While the responses of returning women to their educational undertakings can run the gamut from terror to exhilaration, it is essential that continuing educators remain sensitive to the range of feelings and reac-

---

I wish to express my thanks to Jane Munro, a doctoral student in adult education at the University of British Columbia and a noted poet, for her superb contribution, the poem, "Hyacinth."

tions that learners may internalize or manifest. The following poem, written especially for this volume, captures the essence of the reentry experience by heightening awareness of the vicissitudes that can accompany a return to formal education.

Hyacinth

Basting the faces together, just to try this place
on for size. Basting stitches. Basting in my own fat,
that's what. The best place here's the coffee shop.
All the pretty girls don't have kids at home,
and the gray-haired, super-natural women scare me.
They've thought about too much. It shows
in their choice of shoes. My shoulder hurts—
this bag's too heavy. In the registrar's office
they told me You've got all deficiencies!
No grade point average. No math. No science.
No foreign language. No English composition.
No employer's name. No spouse to speak of.
As if deficiencies were badges. As if I'd earned them.

No softness in my voice. That cuticle's bleeding again.
They're polite to me, but no one has the slightest idea
of the mess in the kitchen or the kid with bronchitis.
What did she mean, *reentry woman?* I never had the chance
to be here before. Too many shadowy hours they'd never dream
it cost to clean, care, cook, cope. Women's work
turned to the inside. Blind hems. Hidden seams.
Who counts the thousand stitches it takes to make
a deficient life? One that doesn't fit anymore.
Swelled head, he said. Sore head's more like it.

It's true—I want more: more than his mother, or mine.
Is that a crime? Mama left me her gold thimble: an
inheritance from her mother. It's not that I think
I'm better. Good women, daughters of farm women,
raised in the church. At sixteen, grandma put her hair up
and wore long skirts. At sixteen, mama embroidered linens.
At sixteen, I made that green dress and failed math.
My only farm's the windowsill. Still, by the time I was
nineteen, I had a daughter, and a husband. There's been
plenty of growing-up around me. *Deficiencies?*
Maybe. To some. But raising kids gives you persistence,
and what I want is what I'd like for them.

Last night, I heard the hyacinth crack its plastic pot.
A root clawed through the green shell.
I heard a crackling, scratching, breaking sound—
thought some black beetle was hatching in there and would
crawl out—but it was just this one white root-tip
lengthening through the split it made.
No needle. No thimble. Just that thread.
Ate a peephole, then let her rip—the coiled growth
from inside straightened out, nosing into space.
Tree roots heave paved roads.
Seed leaves lift pebbles.
The blind morning glory rises through
cement step, baseboard, window frame,
climbs summer long inside the front hall.
Such common, vulnerable threads of life.

All deficiencies? Reentry? The force that drives
a hyacinth root comes from its ups and downs, the years it
blossomed and sank. I'm going to show the kids—anyone who
looks—that just because you're vulnerable
doesn't mean you're weak.
Made, mended, remade. A thimble's
a tiny cup, a shining cap. Mama would push me into this
if she could. Perhaps that's reentry—generations
packed into my head and heart, a full bulb, freshly planted.

Jane Munro, 1988

Themes and Issues

While research in the area of female adult development remains relatively unexplored, the developmental concerns of women in their middle years have been well delineated by the contributors to this sourcebook. Tarule (Chapter Two) poignantly expresses the idea that what returning women want and need is an education in which connection is emphasized over separation, understanding over judgment, and collaboration over debate. She articulately emphasizes women's need for a system that helps them to define their own questions and develop their own patterns of work, rather than one that imposes its own expectations and arbitrary requirements. Lewis (Chapter One) helps to operationalize this philosophy by suggesting ways in which institutions, agencies, and programs can develop practices and policies that are responsive to women's educational needs and personal concerns. Although the reality is sometimes different from the ideal, the exemplary practices in higher education detailed in Copland's (Chapter Three) informative discussion of institutional and programmatic supports for returning women suggest that effective models do exist and can be replicated.

Watkins's (Chapter Four) focus on attentiveness of the corporate sector to women's workplace requirements helps to broaden the perspective on returning women. Her thoughtful delineation of innovative policies and practices in private industry calls attention to the often underrepresented but important corporate point of view. The long-range goal of many reentry women is to obtain employment upon completion of their educational programs, and business and industry linkages can serve not only to facilitate communication between education and the private sector but also to promote increased understanding of the needs of adult learners.

Howell and Schwartz (Chapter Five) also emphasize the importance of joint ventures with industry for enhancing employment opportunities for reentry women. They offer keen insights into the issues confronting women pursing nontraditional careers. Their description of the comprehensive role played by community-based organizations serves as a reminder that the educational progression from basic skills training to employment can be long and strenuous, and that the numerous obstacles facing women entering nontraditional fields require tenacity on the part of the trainees and the organization. The same perseverance predominates for the women of color, the rural dwellers, the displaced homemakers, and the physically challenged women that Safman (Chapter Six) describes. Her articulate synthesis becomes the capstone of the sourcebook, as she enhances our awareness of the unique concerns of special populations of returning women. Clearly, the contributions of these authors broaden the base of understanding we require for developing meaningful supports for reentry women participating in a variety of learning environments.

Institutional and Personal Supports: Where to Draw the Line?

For women returning to school, engaging in formal education often means a disruption in established routines, family life, and friendships. It is not uncommon to find significant others, coworkers, employers, relatives, and spouses opposed to a woman's educational undertaking. There are husbands who fear that a wife's return to formal education will affect the relationship and cause the couple to grow apart. There are family members who question time spent away from home that would normally have been dedicated to domestic responsibilities. The logistics of time may challenge traditional parental roles, as studying and class attendance are balanced against home responsibilities. In combination with the multiple pressures that already accompany a return to school, for some reentry women the added stress can prove devastating.

Numerous researchers have observed that a partner's attitude toward a woman's return to school is a crucial factor in her educational success and satisfaction (Hooper, 1979; DeGroot, 1980; Gilbert, 1982; Lewis, 1983). While many women elicit a high degree of support and enthusiasm from significant others, others encounter passive nonsupport, resistance, and even open hostility in response to their educational aspirations. In addition, the degree of initial support can change as the realities of the educational experience take precedence over original conceptions of what would be. Thus, high initial support may later be replaced by resistance, as long-distance commuting, extended hours at the library, and lack of free time become the norm.

Attitudinal, emotional, and functional supports, or their lack, are most frequently reported in the literature as affecting educational participation. *Attitudinal support* reflects others' traditional or nontraditional perspectives on appropriate roles for women. Attitudinal measures of support assess the extent to which one agrees or disagrees with the roles a woman chooses to assume or abandon. *Emotional support* involves approval or disapproval of a woman's educational goals and is the degree of support she receives from others, including children, friends, significant others, employers, classmates, and the like. *Functional support* is a measure of the division of labor and household responsibilities—that extent to which others assume and share in the chores, given the woman's return to school. Each category speaks to a different dimension of the term *support* and is a unique criterion for measuring the extent to which support does or does not exist.

Given what are commonly referred to as *changing times*, some people question whether there really are women who experience lack of support from significant others. The fact is that support, whether attitudinal, emotional, or functional, continues to loom as a large issue for many returning women. Caution should be used in generalizing, but research spanning the past twenty-five years indicates that a woman's decision to return to school continues to be questioned and challenged by significant others, and that minimal changes in traditional allocations of domestic responsibility have occurred (Houle, 1961; Astin, 1976; Lewis, 1981).

A study of the attitudes and behavior of the spouses of women attending public and private institutions of higher education was conducted recently to determine how educational planners could gain a better understanding of home support in order to improve future educational opportunities for women (Valentine and others, 1987). The researchers identified conceptually distinct types of women, who differed with respect to the nature and amount of support they experienced. They ranged from women who received emotional and logistical support to those who experienced subtle and overt forms of sabotage.

My own research with low-literate adults returning to school reveals

Figure 1. Taxonomy of Supporters and Countersupporters

Supporters

    Rooters
        People who encourage learners in their efforts

    Resources
        People who assist learners by providing services and information

    Challengers
        Critical evaluators, role models, and mentors who sponsor learners and push them even farther

Countersupporters

    Constants
        People who like learners just the way they are and do not want them to change

    Toxics
        People who put learners down and inhibit their efforts

Source: Lewis, 1985.

similar findings and suggests how negative support can affect attendance and success (Lewis, 1985). During interviews with over two-hundred currently enrolled adult basic students, respondents could readily identify supporters and countersupporters who contributed to or detached from their educational programs. For those students who experienced countersupport, the most negative reactions came from family members and friends. Significant others made up the largest group of individuals who encouraged students to remain as they were and not to return to school. Black and Hispanic students reported the greatest number of countersupporters, while single, widowed, separated, and divorced students had significantly fewer positive supporters than married students did. To exacerbate an already negative situation, those who experienced countersupport identified significantly more countersupporters than did those with positive supports. Thus, negativity was found to beget negativity. In fact, women without supporters continually expressed concern about their ability to persevere in the face of negative feedback and opposition.

Figure 1 depicts the taxonomy that was developed to assist students in identifying those who had either positive or negative impacts on their participation in continuing education. A similar taxonomy could be easily used by others interested in determining both the type and range of supports available to returning women.

Translating Research into Practice

Studies such as the one described here change our conception of high-risk students. When we move beyond the demographic variables (such as gender, age, race, marital status, and educational attainment) that are commonly used to identify high-risk groups, support is seen to be a significant factor in assessing for success in continuing education. Certain individuals may be in jeopardy of stopping out or dropping out on the basis of lack of personal support. Moreover, we must direct attention to those who need additional institutional support and services.

Related literature suggests that different agents of support are needed over the life cycle, and that the primary agents of support change over time (Tamir and Antonucci, 1981). While friends may be a better buffer for traditional-aged women enrolling in educational programs directly after high school, the support of significant others (spouses, children, relatives, employers, teachers, coworkers) may be even more important for returning women (Roehl and Okun, 1984). Therefore, it behooves educational providers to ensure that a variety of resources and services are in place to help counterbalance the negative pressures that may be exerted on learners. When returning women are helped to expand their social networks and identify resources outside their immediate families and friends, their reliance on significant others as the sole source of support can be reduced.

This objective sounds reasonable, but it is not easily achieved. The difficulty in discussing support with returning women is that the issue is emotionally charged. Many women are embarrased to discuss a personal situation, feeling that it jeopardizes their viability as serious students and their egalitarian status in relation to their male counterparts. Others sublimate the issue and shy away from the idea of support groups or counseling sessions that could expose their vulnerability to external pressures. Thus, the very services that could be most beneficial are sometimes rejected because the level of comfort required for revealing one's personal situation has not developed.

Reentry women are less likely than traditional-aged students to make use of available services (Bandenhoop and Johansen, 1980; Kasworm, 1980). Numerous reasons have been advanced for this behavior; several factors may contribute to women's underutilization of support services. One possibility is that returning women, who are primarily part-time attendees, are not privy to the same informal networks that traditional-aged students use. Thus, lack of information, and a feeling that services are inappropriate or geared to younger students, may preclude participation. Repeated encouragement and exposure by staff and faculty to the plethora of available options may be necessary before resources are tapped.

Recommendations

To provide a hospitable environment for reentry women, the following recommendations are offered as examples of good practice. The suggestions also underscore the premise that responsibility for successful reentry programming rests with the student, as well as with the institution or organization.

Develop an Open-Door Policy. Family members and friends, along with anyone who questions what goes on in the educational setting, should be encouraged to visit classes, meet teachers, and participate in visiting days or orientation sessions. This will not only help to debunk some of the existing myths about education but will also allow those who feel excluded to experience the educational environment firsthand. In some instances, it may mean that significant others will become the target population for outreach activities and publicity campaigns, not just returning women themselves.

Encourage Support Groups. Opportunities should be made available for individuals to work together with peers so that linkages can be developed and school-based support can be established. Assignments should be structured so as to allow learners the option of working alone, in dyads, or in groups. The more opportunities returning women have to connect with others, the greater the chances of compensating for externally imposed negative attitudes or discouragement. Returning women need to establish friendships with others in similar situations who share common concerns. Ensuring that there is a conveniently located room or lounge where part-time students can meet and talk is one way of encouraging networks.

Develop a Holistic Perspective. The experiences of returning women, including their familial and personal concerns, must be considered as integral parts of the educational process, directly related to persistence patterns. It is not sufficient merely to teach classes without gaining a fuller understanding of the issues that trouble students. Educators are encouraged to talk with learners to determine what additional support services would be beneficial and to ascertain how external pressure can be minimized.

Stagger Orientation Sessions. While orientations and get-acquainted sessions are commonly offered upon initial entry into an educational program, sessions throughout the year would provide additional chances for those who disregarded earlier opportunities to participate. As individuals proceed beyond the status of newcomer, their needs change, as does their readiness to engage with others. Once learners become comfortable and more familiar with the system, they are better able to identify what they need to do for themselves in order to succeed.

Sensitize Staff and Faculty. Counselors, teachers, administrators, and staff should be encouraged to learn as much as they can about the needs of returning women in order to develop responsive behavior, services, and programs. Information on personal and cross-cultural variables that may be impeding participation should be shared through professional-development sessions, small-group meetings, and related research and literature. Visits to other educational settings with model programs should also be encouraged.

Create Alternate Routes to Learning. In addition to offering courses one day a week, late afternoons, and evenings, newer scheduling alternatives should be made available. Weekend colleges, intensive summer institutes, cooperative education and internships, and external degree programs are just a few of the many possibilities. Classes should be offered at convenient off-campus locations, as well as through telecommunication networks. Credit and noncredit offerings, including career-development courses, refresher classes, how-to sessions, and direction-finding workshops, should be available on a continuing basis. Whether the need is for community-oriented non-credit programming, certificate programs, continuing education units, or academic or job-oriented programs, the goal is to develop methods and curricula that are based on the defined needs of learners.

Develop Institutional Commitment. Ensure that there is participation at all levels in planning programs for returning women. Institutional support that depends solely on volunteers or on a select few is tenuous. Therefore, it is important to offer compensation, provide released time, and create additional positions to support programs for returning women. To guarantee that institutional policies are not working at cross-purposes, and that special-interest groups within the reentry population are considered, a reentry coordinator should be appointed.

Evaluate Continually. Because the characteristics of the reentry population may change from year to year, periodic evaluations must be implemented to determine who the actual reentry participants are and what they perceive their needs to be. This means that ongoing needs assessment, surveys, and interviews with past, current, and potential participants must be conducted in order to evaluate whether changes in curricular or institutional structures are necessary.

Remain on the Cutting Edge. Women should be able to avail themselves of many options and services designed to encourage their continuing participation. These may include dorms for single parents; reserved floors in graduate residences for older students; life-skills seminars organized around psychological-adjustment themes; one-stop academic, personal, and career counseling; block scheduling for returning women; or simply the publication of a reentry student survival guide.

Assess Your Readiness. The following questions, adapted from those posed by the Project on the Status and Education of Women, are a way of determining whether an institution or organization is prepared to respond to the needs of returning women (Fisher Thompson, 1981) Affirmative responses suggest that a philosophical commitment has been made, which can serve as a strong foundation for supporting the needs of returning women, as well as those of a variety of other special-needs constituencies.

- Have you examined your present policies to make sure that they do not exclude, even unintentionally, any group of potential students?
- Do all the policies, even though ostensibly fair, have a disproportionate effect on older students, especially women?
- Are there written policies that are formulated on the fair treatment of all students, and have these policies been made clear to all constituents?
- Has an effort been made to expand recruitment to nontraditional students?
- Have you done your best to discover and respond to the concerns of this new population of returning students?

Selected Resources for Returning Women

The central goal of reentry programming is to help women see themselves and their relationships in new ways by taking responsibility for their lives, examining past options, and formulating new plans. The following is a list of organizations and agencies that can be of assistance in the realization of that goal.

American Association for Adult and Continuing Education
1201 16th Street, N.W., Suite 230
Washington, D.C. 90036
(202)463-6333

American Association for Higher Education
One Dupont Circle, N.W., Suite 600
Washington, D.C. 20036
(202)293-6440

American Association of Retired Persons—Women's Division
1909 K Street, N.W.
Washington, D.C. 20049
(202)872-4700

American Association of University Women
Educational Foundations Program
2401 Virginia Avenue, N.W.
Washington, D.C. 20037
(202)785-7700

American Association of Women in Community and Junior Colleges
3049 N. 6th Street, P.O. Box 908
LaCrosse, Wisconsin 54602
(608)785-9101

American Council of the Blind
1010 Vermont Avenue, N.W., Suite 1100
Washington, D.C. 20005
(202)393-3666

American Council on Education—Office of Women
in Higher Education and Office of Educational Credit
One Dupont Circle, N.W.
Washington, D.C. 20036
(202)939-9300

Americans for Indian Opportunity
2001 19th Street, N.W.
Washington, D.C. 20036
(202)371-1280

Association on Handicapped Student Service Programs
in Postsecondary Education
P.O. Box 21192
Columbus, Ohio 43221
(614)488-4972

Business and Professional Women's Foundation
2012 Massachusetts Avenue, N.W.
Washington, D.C. 20036
(202)293-1200

Council for Adult and Experiential Learning
10840 Little Patuxent Parkway, Suite 203
Columbia, Maryland 21044
(301)997-3535

Displaced Homemakers Network
1411 K Street, N.W., Suite 930
Washington, D.C. 20005
(202)628-6767

League of United Latin American Citizens—Women's Division
400 First Street, N.W., Suite 721
Washington, D.C. 20011
(202)628-0717

Links, Inc.
1200 Massachusetts Avenue, N.W.
Washington, D.C. 20005
(202)842-8686

Mexican American Women's National Association
1201 16th Street, N.W., Suite 420
Washington, D.C. 20036
(202)223-3440

National Association of Commissions for Women
YWCA Building, Suite M-10
624 9th Street, N.W.
Washington, D.C. 20001
(202)628-5030

National Association of University Women
1205 W. 80th Street
Los Angeles, California 90044
(213)753-7572

National Association of Women Deans, Administrators and Counselors
1325 18th Street, N.W., #210
Washington, D.C. 20036
(202)659-9330

National Commission on Working Women
1325 G Street, N.W., Lower Level
Washington, D.C. 20005
(202)737-5764

National Congress of Neighborhood Women
249 Manhattan Avenue
Brooklyn, New York 11211
(718)388-6666

National Educational Association
1201 16th Street, N.W.
Washington, D.C. 20036
(202)833-4000

National Institute for Women of Color
P.O. Box 50583
Washington, D.C. 20004
(202)828-0735

National Society for Internships and Experiential Education
122 St. Mary's Street
Raleigh, North Carolina 27605
(919)834-7536

National University Continuing Education Association
One Dupont Circle, N.W., Suite 420
Washington, D.C. 20036
(202)659-3130

National Women's Education Fund
2000 P Street, N.W., Suite 515
Washington, D.C. 20036
(202)822-6636

National Women's Student Coalition
c/o U.S. Student Association
1012 14th Street, N.W., Suite 403
Washington, D.C. 20005
(202)775-8943

Older Women's League
1325 G Street, N.W., Lower Level B
Washington, D.C. 20005
(202)783-6686

Project on Equal Education Rights
1333 H Street, N.W., 11th Floor
Washington, D.C. 20005
(202)682 0940

Project on the Status and Education of Women
1818 R Street, N.W.
Washington, D.C. 20009
(202)387-1300

Rural American Women
Route 2, Box 235
Kempton, Pennsylvania, 19529
(215)756-6362

U.S. Department of Education
Graduate and Professional Study Fellowships
400 Maryland Avenue, S.W., Room 3060
Washington, D.C. 20202
(202)732-3366

U.S. Department of Labor—Women's Bureau
200 Constitution Avenue, N.W.
Washington, D.C. 20210
(202)523-6611

Wider Opportunities for Women
1325 G Street, N.W., Lower Level
Washington, D.C. 20005
(202)638-3143

Women's College Coalition
1101 17th Street, N.W., Suite 1001
Washington, D.C. 20036
(202)466-5430

References

Astin, H. S. (ed.). *Some Action of Her Own: The Adult Woman and Higher Education.* Lexington, Mass.: Heath, 1976.

Bandenhoop, M. S., and Johansen, M. K. "Do Re-entry Women Have Special Needs?" *The Counseling Psychologist,* 1980, *4,* 491-595.

DeGroot, S. "Female and Male Returnees: Glimpses of Two Distinct Populations." *Psychology of Women Quarterly,* 1980, *5* (2), 358-362.

Fisher-Thompson, J. *"An Overview of Re-entry Women: Meeting the Enrollment Challenge."* Washington, D.C.: Project on the Status and Education of Women, 1981.

Gilbert, M. G. "The Impact of Graduate School on the Family: A Systems View." *Journal of College Student Personnel,* 1982, *23,* 128-135.

Hooper, J. O. "Returning Women Students and Their Families: Support and Conflict." *Journal of College Student Personnel,* 1979, *20,* 145-152.

Houle, C. *The Inquiring Mind.* Madison: University of Wisconsin Press, 1961.

Kasworm, C. E. "Student Services for the Older Undergraduate Student." *Journal of College Student Personnel,* 1980, *21* (2), 163-169.

Lewis, L. H. "A Study of the Sex-Role Attitudes and Marital Adjustment of Female Doctoral Candidates and Their Spouses During the Course of Doctoral Study." Unpublished doctoral dissertation, Oregon State University, 1981.

Lewis, L. H. "Coping with Change: Married Women in Graduate School." *Lifelong Learning,* 1983, *7* (1), 8-28.

Lewis, L. H. "An Issue of Support." *International Journal of Lifelong Education,* 1985, *4* (2), 163-176.

Roehl, J. E., and Okun, M. A. "Depression Symptoms Among Women Reentering College: The Role of Negative Life Events and Family Social Support." *Journal of College Student Personnel,* 1984, *25,* 251-254.

Tamir, L. M., and Antonucci, T. C. "Self-Perception, Motivation, and Social Support Through the Family Life Course." *Journal of Marriage and the Family,* 1981, *43,* 151-160.

Valentine, T., Hopkins, D. E., Powers-Burdick, P. A., and Schubauer, L. N. "Spouse Support and Sabotage of Adult Women Students." Paper presented at the American Association for Adult and Continuing Education Conference, Washington, D.C., October 1987.

Linda H. Lewis is associate professor of adult education at the University of Connecticut and codirector of the university's Vocational Equity Research, Training, and Evaluation Center.

Index

A

Abused women, 85, 86, 87, 89
Academic counselling, 36, 73, 84
Academic programming, for reentry women, 12-15, 36-37, 45-46, 101-104
Adult College, at Mercyhurst College, 37
Adult-services model programs, 38-39
Affirmative action legislation, 50-51
Alleman, E., 41, 46
Alverno College, 36, 37
American Association for Adult and Continuing Education, 104
American Association for Higher Education, 104
American Association of Retired Persons, 60-61, 104
American Association of University Women, 104
American Association of Women in Community and Junior Colleges, 105
American Council of the Blind, 105
American Council on Education, 105
American Express, 92
American Handicapped Workers Foundation Scholarship, 90
Americans for Indian Opportunity, 105
Anderson, W., 7, 17
Anger management, 81, 82
Antonucci, T. C., 101, 108
Applebaum, F., 50, 51-52, 53-54, 63
Apprenticeship training programs, 54, 62
Askell, E. F., 45, 46
Assertive communication program, 83
Assertiveness training: for Chicana women, 87, 88; for disabled women, 92; for displaced homemakers, 81, 82; for rural women, 85
Association on Handicapped Student Service Programs in Postsecondary Education, 105
Astin, H. S., 6, 15, 99, 108
Attitudinal support, for reentry, 99
Awards and honors, 38-39, 44

B

Baker-Miller, J., 24, 32
Baldwin, P., 58, 63
Bandenhoop, M. S., 13, 16, 101, 108
Bank of America, 56
Baron, J., 57, 63
Basic skills, 14, 69-70, 82, 87
Belenky, M., 20, 21, 22, 32
"Believing game," 2
Benefit programs, in workplace, 54-55, 61, 63
Bergquist, W., 26, 32
Bernstein, A., 55, 56, 61, 63
Beutell, N. J., 7, 16
Black studies, 29
Bloomsbury University, 39
Brice, G., 59-60, 61, 63
Brookfield, S., 28, 32
Bruffee, K., 29, 32
Bryant, D., 19, 32
Buerk, D., 30, 32
Burke, J., 37, 46
Business and professional Women's Foundation, 105

C

Calvin, C., 43, 44, 47
Carbine, J., 79n
Career interruptions, among women, 51-52, 59
Career planning, 36, 81, 84
"Caregivers in the Workplace," 60-61
Caregiving, to the elderly, 59-61
Carnegie Council on Policy Studies in Higher Education, 1, 2
Center for Community Education, at Onondaga Community College, 84-86
Center for Disabled Student Services, 79n, 80, 89-92

111

Center for Women, at University of Toledo, 44
Champion International Corporation, 60
Chatham College, 36, 37
Chicana women, 80, 86-89, 100
Chicken Soup (Minneapolis), 56
Chickering, A., 8, 16
Childcare: in academic programming, 10, 14, 36, 38, 39, 41, 42, 43; as barrier to reentry, 9-10, 13; and special need population, 82, 89, 92; in workplace, 55-56, 58-59, 61
City University of New York system, 42
Clayton, D. E., 6-7, 16
Clinchy, B., 20, 21, 22, 32
Cochran, J. R., 41, 46
Collaborative learning, 21, 31
Collaborative teaching strategies, 1, 29-30
College Without Walls, at Stephens College, 37
Collins, G., 60, 63
Community-based organizational (CBO) training programs, 65-77
Comprehensive Employment and Training Act (1962, 1973) (CETA), 53
Connected learning, 20, 1-22, 23, 25-29, 32
Connecticut Light and Power Company, 71
Connecticut State University system, 42
Consortial development, 93
Constructed knowing, concept of, 22, 31
Cooperative Extension Service, 84
Cooperative learning, 21, 31
Copas, E. M., 43, 46
Copland, B. A., 35-48, 98
Copland-Wood, B. A., 35-48, 98
Cottage industries, 57
Council for Adult and Experiential Learning, 105
Counselling services: in academic programming, 10, 15, 36, 41-42, 102; in CBOs, 72-73; for Chicana women, 87, 88; for displaced homemakers, 81, 82, 83; for rural women, 84, 85; in workplace, 54

Countersupport, for reentry women, 99-100, 101, 102
Creange, R., 9, 16
Critical thinking, 21
Cross, K. P., 8, 16
Curricular strategies, 9-29, 30, 103

D

Dallas Childcare Partnership, 58
Daloz, L., 27, 32
Daniels, L. A., 42, 46
Daubman, K., 40, 47
Dayton Hudson, 56
DeGroot, S., 99, 108
Dependency issues, for reentry women, 82, 83, 85, 86, 92
Dependent Care Assistance Program (1981), 56
Developmental position, concept of, 20, 22, 23, 29-32
Dickerson, K. G., 8, 16
Disabled women, 6, 80, 89-93
Disadvantaged women, 6, 65
Discrimination, 75, 92
Displaced homemakers, 6; in adult education, 9, 13, 43-44; in job training, 52-54, 80-83, 84, 92-93
Displaced Homemakers Network, 9, 16, 105
Displaced Homemakers Project, 80-83, 85
Divinell, P. L., 43, 46
Division of Rehabilitation Services, 90
"Doubting game," 21
Durcholz, P., 6, 16

E

Earnings capacity, 51-52, 53-54
Earnings gap, 51-52
Edinboro University, 36, 37
Educating Rita, 19, 23-24, 26, 27, 28
Elbow, P., 21, 22, 32
Elder Caregiver's Project, 49, 59-60, 61-62
Emotional support, for reentry women, 99
Empty-nest syndrome, 6
ENCORE, at University of North Carolina, 42

Equity stage, of institutional adaptation, 45
Ethnic harassment, 75
Even, W., 52, 63

F

Fairhaven College, at Western Washington University, 37
Federal aid programs, 13
Financial aid, 10, 13, 14; in academic programs, 37, 38, 39, 43
First Bank System, 56
Fisher-Thompson, J., 12, 16, 103, 108
Flextime, 57, 61
Freire, 26
Functional support, for reentry women, 99

G

Gateway Program, at Chatham College, 36, 37
GED program, 87
Georgia State University, 41
Gerber, B., 61, 63
Gibeau, J., 60, 63
Gilbert, M. G., 99, 108
Gilder, G., 51, 63
Gilligan, C., 7, 16, 20, 32
Goddard College, 43
Goldberg, G., 38, 40, 46
Goldberg, J., 79n
Goldberg, N., 20, 21, 22, 32
Grading system, academic, 15, 37, 41
Great Depression, 50
Great Valley Corporate Center, 60
Green, M., 26, 32
Greenberg, E., 26, 32
Greenfeig, B., 38, 40, 46
Greenhaus, J. H., 7, 16
Griffith, J., 30, 33
Grotthau, B., 16

H

Hacker, A., 53, 63
Hall, L., 42, 46
Hall, R., 8, 13, 16, 21, 33
Hartford Area Training Center (HATC), 67, 69, 70, 74-75
Hartford College for Women, 67, 71, 75

Hartford job-skills training network, 74-75
Hartford State Technical College, 71
Havighurst, R., 8, 16
Hay, J., 58, 59
Hewlett-Packard, 57
Hill, S. T., 1, 2
Hinkle, D. E., 8, 16
Hispanic women, 80, 86-89, 100
Home support, for reentry women, 98-101
Hood College, 37
Hooper, J. O., 99, 108
Hopkins, D. E., 99, 108
Houle, C., 99, 108
Housing, for reentry women, 15, 43
"How Companies Help," 55, 63
Howell, R. S., 65-77, 98
"Hyacinth," 95n, 96-97

I

Identity-line tension, 7-8
Illini Symposia for Women, 38
Illinois State University, 39
Indiana University, 39
Indiana University of Pennsylvania, 39
Institute for Research on Poverty, 51
Institutional adaptation, to reentry students, 41, 45-46, 101-104
Institutional support, for reentry women, 101
Intergenerational day care, 60
International Business Machines (IBM), 60, 92
Internships, 36, 37, 70
Interviewing skills, 81, 83, 84, 87, 88

J

Jacklin, C., 8, 17
Jacobs, S. B., 41, 46
Job-seeking skills classes, 75-76; for Chicana women, 87, 88; for displaced homemakers, 81, 83; for rural women, 84. *See also* Assertiveness training
Job sharing, 57
Job Training Partnership Act (JTPA), 62, 68; Chicana women and, 87, 88; displaced homemakers and, 53, 81; rural women and, 84

Johansen, M. K., 13, 16, 101, 108
Jovacchini, E., 42, 46

K

Kahn, H., 50, 57, 59, 63
Kamerman, S., 54, 55, 57, 63
Kanter, 61
Kasworm, C. E., 13, 16, 101, 108
Kelson, V., 79n
Kennedy, J. M., 58, 63
Kimbrell, C. D., 46
Kingston, P., 54, 55, 57, 63
Kramarae, C., 21, 33

L

L & N School, 49, 58-59
LaGuardia Community College, 39
Laissez-faire stage, of institutional adaptation, 45
League of United Latin American Citizens, 105
"Learning backwards," 26-27
Learning strategies, 21-22, 26-30
Leppell, K., 8, 17
Levin, E. L., 41, 46
Lewis, J. S., 37, 46
Lewis, L. H., 5-18, 95-109
Links, Inc., 106
Literacy skills, 82, 87, 69-70
Littrell, D. P., 37, 46
Lomas and Nettleton, 58-59, 61-62
Louise Snow Scholarship, 90

M

Maccoby, E., 8, 17
Magid, R., 56, 63
Maher, F., 29, 33
Mahoney, C., 7, 17
Mair, D., 79n
Mardoyan, J. L., 41, 46
Martin, J. R., 24, 33
Maslin, A., 6, 7, 17
Mature Students program, at University of South Carolina, 38, 39, 40
Mayor's childcare task force of Dallas, 58
Mercyhurst College, 37
Merkel, J., 79n

Mexican American Women's National Association, 106
Mi Casa Resource Center for Women, 79n, 80, 86-89
Mills, D., 43, 44, 47
Mills College, 42
Minorities, ethnic and racial, 6, 13, 80, 86-89, 92, 100
Moore, W., 36, 47
Multidisciplinary Center for the Study of Aging, at State University of New York, 59-60
Multiple role responsibility, 7-8
Munro, J., 95n, 96-97

N

Nadeau, O., 79n
Nassau Community College, 39
National Association of Counties, 86
National Association for the Education of Young Children, 58
National Association of University Women, 106
National Association for Women, 106
National Association of Women Deans, Administrators and Counselors, 106
National Commission on Working Women, 106
National Congress of Neighborhood Women, 106
National Educational Association, 106
National Institute for Women of Color, 106
National Longitudinal Survey of Mature Women, 51
National Society for Internships and Experiential Education, 107
National University Continuing Education Association, 107
National Women's Education Fund, 107
National Women's Student Coalition, 107
Network intervention program, 40
New York State Department of Education, 83
New York State Division of Human Rights, 84
Nielson, M., 79n

Nontraditional training programs, 65–77
Northern Michigan University, 39
Nowak, C., 59

O

Occupational Safety and Health Administration, 76
O'Conner, J., 6, 16
O'Donnell, K., 26, 32
Office of the Dean of Studies, at University of Texas, 38, 39
Office of Women's Resources and Services, at University of Illinois, 38
Okun, M. A., 101, 108
Older women, 6, 13
Older Women's League, 107
Onondaga Child Care Council, 84
Onondaga Community College, 80, 83–86
Onondaga County Employment and Training Agency, 84
On-the-job training, 54, 62
Open-door policy, 102
Open-entry, open-exit model, 72
Opportunity College, at Edinboro University, 36–37
Orientation, academic, 10, 36, 102; in academic programs, 37, 38, 39–41
Outstanding Adult Student Award, 38, 39

P

Part-time employment, 57, 61, 63
Part-time enrollment, of reentry women, 1, 8; in academic programs, 37, 39; accommodating, 12–13, 14, 15, 101
Patrick, J., 79n
Pedagogic strategies, 28–29, 30
Peer support, 40
Pell Grants, 90
Pennsylvania State University, 38, 39, 40, 41, 42, 44
Pepsico, 60
Perry, W., 29, 33
Personal and situational barriers, to reentry, 8–12
Pfeffer, J., 57, 63
Philadelphia Banks, 56

Phillips, M., 40, 47
Phoenix Institute, 79n, 80–83
Placement, in workplace, 74–76
Postsecondary education, for reentry women, 1, 35–46
Powers-Burdick, P.A., 99, 108
Precision Machining Training Program, 69
Preview Privilege Program, at Hood College, 37
Private Industry Council (Connecticut), 74–75
Procedural knowing, concept of, 22, 31
Project on Equal Education Rights, 107
Project on the Status and Education of Women, 103, 107
Project Succeed, at University of Toledo, 44
Prospect Associates, 56

Q

Quintilliani, D. W., 5n, 10–12

R

Received knowing, concept of, 22, 29, 30, 31
Recruitment, of reentry women, 13, 36, 66–68, 81
Reentry, defined, 5–10, 79–80
Relationship: in learning, 21, 22, 24–29, 31; and reentry support, 99–101
Remediation, for basic skills, 69–70
Remington Products, Inc., 60
Respite program, 60
Resume preparation, 81, 83, 84, 87
"Retention services," for CBO graduates, 76
Retraining, in workplace, 54, 62
Returning Adult Student Center, at Pennsylvania State University, 38, 39, 44
Roehl, J. F., 101, 108
Rogers, C., 25, 33
Ruddick, S., 24, 33
Rural American Women, 107
Rural women, 6, 80, 83–86, 92–93
Rural Women's Work Readiness Project, 79n, 80, 83–86

S

Safman, P. C., 79-94, 98
Sandler, B., 21, 33
Scheduling, academic: in academic planning, 13, 14, 15, 103; in academic programs, 36, 37
Schubauer, L. N., 99, 108
Schwartz, H., 65-77, 98
Scott, N. A., 35-36, 47
Seawell, M., 31, 33
Second Chance program, at University of Lowell, 37
Second Wind program, at University of Maryland, 38
Seear, B. N., 52, 54, 63
Self-advocacy, 73
Self-esteem, 8-12; among Chicana women, 87, 88; among disabled women, 90-92, 93; among displaced homemakers, 82, 83; among rural women, 85, 86
Self-reflection, 28-29
Separate thinking, 28
Separatist stage, of institutional adaptation, 45
Service occupations, 50
Sexual harassment, 75, 76
"Shadowing," in training programs, 70
Shaw, G. B., 19, 33
Silence, concept of, 22, 25, 31
Single Parent Project, at Goddard College, 43
Single parents, 6, 7-8, 9, 13, 43
Skills assessment, 81, 84, 87
Skills training, nontraditional, 65-77
Smith, M. M., 6-7, 16
Snyder, D. T., 1, 3
Social Security Disability Insurance, 90
Southeast Missouri State University, 39
Southwestern Bell Telephone Company, 60
State University of New York, 59-60
Stautberg, S., 56, 57, 62, 64
Steelcase, Inc., 57
Stephens College, 37
Stevens, B., 25, 33
Stride Rite Corporation, 60
Striegel-Moore, R., 41, 46
Student organizations, for reentry women, 44-45
Subjective knowing, concept of, 22, 31
Support groups, 41-42, 83, 85, 87, 102
Support services, 13, 101; academic planning for, 10, 14, 15, 36, 102, 103; in academic programs, 37, 38, 39, 41-42, 43-44; in CBOs, 68-69; for disabled women, 93. *See also* Childcare; Counselling services; Job-seeking skills classes
Swift, J. S., 43, 44, 47
"Symposium on Aging," 61, 64

T

Tamir, L. M., 101, 108
Tarule, J. M., 19-34, 97
Television, in recruitment, 81
Temporary work, 63
3M Corporation, 56
Travelers Insurance Corporation, 59-60
Tutorials, 36, 37

U

Unger, D. G., 41, 46
Unions, 62
U.S. Bureau of the Census, 1, 3, 12, 49, 50, 56
U.S. Department of Education, 107
U.S. Department of Labor, 9, 50, 56, 64, 108
United Way, 81, 87
University of Alabama, 39
University of Georgia, 39, 43
University of Illinois, 38
University of Lowell, 37
University of Maryland, 38, 40-41
University of North Carolina, 42
University of South Carolina, 38, 39, 40, 41-42
University of Tennessee, 39
University of Texas, 38, 39, 40
University of Toledo, 44
University of Utah, 80, 89-92
University of Wisconsin, 42-43, 51
Utah Displaced Homemakers Act (1986), 80, 81, 82

V

Valentine, T., 99, 108
Vocational counselling, 54
Voice, concept of, 20-21, 23-25, 26, 29, 31, 32

W

Walker, L., 85, 94
Warmline, at University of Maryland, 38
Watkins, K. E., 49-64, 98
Weekend College, at Alverno College, 36, 37
Welin, C., 58, 64
Western Washington University, 37
Whatley, A. E., 15, 17
Widener University, 40

Wider Opportunities for Women, 69, 108
Wilmoth, D., 40, 47
Women's College Coalition, 108
Women's Opportunity Network (WON), at University of Georgia, 43
Women's studies, 29
Work-at-home options, 57
Workforce, reentry into, 49-63
Work-study program, 13, 43
World of Work (WOW), 74, 75-76

Y

YMCA, 56
YWCA, 84
Yogev, S., 7, 17
Yohalem, A., 50, 53, 54, 62, 64